2025
PODCAST
PLAYBOOK

Compiled and Edited By Rob Staggenborg, APR, MS

Media Strategist, Podcast Consultant, Content Creator

Copyright Notice

For Adam, Nick, Logan, Amanda
Dave, Judy, Paige, Rose, Isaac
and our Stand Tall team

"Your voice is your power. Use it to inspire, influence, and ignite change."

Oprah Winfrey

Disclaimer

Contents

Author's Note

"Do you want an iPod with your computer?"

I remember vividly the time I first encountered the concept of this new gadget they called the iPod. It sure was a sight. Big and bulky, it was roughly the size of a cigarette pack if anyone is old enough to remember those. The iPod had a big dial on the front of it, and you scrolled by spinning the dial in a circular motion. By today's standards it is quite archaic, but at the time it was just fantastic.

The back of the iPod was a thing of beauty in itself; it was chrome silver, smooth and just the coolest thing you ever held in your hand.

The music was great too. My first iPod I managed to cram 4.7 days of music … days! I burned so many

CDs, the 80s hair band Firehouse was ringing in my ears. It was just the craziest invention I'd ever encountered.

But in terms of its usefulness - back in 2000? Not much. It was gadgety and cool, but barely resembled the iPods and its younger brothers, the iPads and iPhones of today.

I initially declined his offer but the special his computer sales company was running included this new gadget called an iPod with the purchase of the mammoth iMac.

Little did I know that 25 years later I would compile and pen a book about this thing called *podcasting*.

As we will learn inside, podcasting was so much more than the iPod, but that little silver gadget helped bring the world of podcasting into the pockets of everyone around the globe.

Sports radio helped me pass the mind-numbing days of communications work. I enjoyed so many things about it. The banter, the updates, the breaking news, the opinion, the interviews with my favorite stars … I loved it all. I was relegated to a lonely office away from almost everything. It had previously served as a bedroom for visiting Christian Brothers, the religious order that ran my old high school. The office was cleared of the bedroom and furniture, however, the sink was still attached solidly to the wall.

For hours upon hours, I would listen to the conversations. As a former journalist, I was a news junkie at heart, and this world of radio and interview shows had me hooked right away.

I ended up becoming a radio producer for a show called **Mind Games, the Psychology of Sports** with Tom Michler and board producer Matt Grover on KFNS 590 AM in Webster Groves, Missouri.

Every Saturday, I'd drive across town to the KFNS studios, where we would record segments and also do a live Saturday morning show. It was a lot of fun, but there was also a mind-blowing amount of technology it took to get each show off the ground. I thank Tom for giving me the opportunity and Matt for teaching me how cool the broadcasting business was.

I hope you are able to learn more about podcasting, learn about some popular shows, and learn now to start your own podcast.

For me, I've grown so much as a podcast host, a podcast guest, a podcast producer and now a podcast consultant. I truly enjoy passing along my knowledge to other aspiring podcasters.

It is a tricky road for some, but with some basic equipment and a lot of ambition, you too can find a niche market for your own podcast.

Good luck and remember … Don't be so hard on yourself! There was only one perfect man and they nailed him to a cross! Be your own biggest fan.

Good luck!

Rob Staggenborg, APR

Introduction

Great … Another Podcast??

Introduction

Like it or not, podcasting is here to stay. It's not going anywhere anytime soon.

Podcasting has revolutionized how we consume information and entertainment. From commuting to cooking dinner to talking about sports, we have access to compelling stories, thought-provoking discussions, and practical insights—all at the touch of a button.

What started as a niche medium for tech-savvy hobbyists has grown into a global powerhouse that influences industries, reshapes cultural norms, and fosters intimate connections between creators and listeners.

This book is your gateway to understanding and thriving in this complex, dynamic world.

The word *podcast* first emerged in 2004, a blend of "iPod" and "broadcast," capturing the essence of this new form of audio communication.

While the term may have originated as a nod to Apple's iconic device, podcasting has since transcended its technological roots.

Today, the medium encompasses a vast ecosystem of creators, platforms, and listeners that spans the globe. With more than 500 million people tuning in to podcasts monthly and millions of shows available in every imaginable genre, podcasting is no longer just a trend—it's a cultural movement.

Why Podcasting Matters

At its core, podcasting is about storytelling and connection. Unlike traditional forms of media, podcasts invite listeners into an intimate, often unfiltered space. Whether it's a solo host sharing personal anecdotes, a gripping investigative series, or a panel of experts debating critical issues, podcasts create a sense of closeness that few other mediums can replicate.

This unique intimacy has made podcasting a favorite for creators and audiences alike, fostering communities around shared interests and ideas.

Podcasting is also remarkably versatile. Creators have the freedom to explore niche topics, experiment with formats, and build authentic relationships with their audiences.

From true crime to business strategy, from comedy to mental health, there's a podcast for everyone.

This diversity has democratized content creation, allowing voices from all backgrounds to be heard. In a world increasingly dominated by visual media, podcasts offer a refreshing alternative: a space where the power of the spoken word takes center stage.

The Numbers Speak for Themselves

The statistics behind podcasting's rise are staggering. In 2023, Edison Research reported that 42% of Americans aged 12 and older listened to podcasts monthly, a number that continues to grow. Globally, podcasting's reach is expanding even faster.

Markets in Europe, Asia, and Latin America have seen double-digit growth rates in listener adoption. Advertising revenue is also booming, with the global podcast ad market projected to exceed $4 billion by 2025.

These numbers underscore podcasting's evolution from a hobbyist activity to a professional and commercial force. For businesses, it's a chance to reach audiences in a deeply personal way.

For creators, it's an opportunity to turn passion projects into viable careers. And for listeners, it's an endless buffet of stories, ideas, and perspectives that enrich daily life.

Why This Book?

Whether you're a seasoned podcaster, an aspiring creator, or simply a curious listener, this book is designed to guide you through every aspect of podcasting.

You'll learn about the history of the medium, explore its current landscape, and gain practical tools for navigating its future. More importantly, you'll discover what makes podcasting such a powerful and transformative medium.

For aspiring podcasters, this book offers a step-by-step roadmap to launching your show. From choosing a format and defining your niche to mastering the technical aspects of recording and editing, you'll find everything you need to get started.

We'll also delve into branding, audience engagement, and monetization—essential components for building a sustainable podcasting career.

For business professionals, this book explores how podcasting can elevate your brand and expand your reach. Whether you're considering starting a branded podcast or sponsoring existing shows, you'll gain insights into leveraging the medium effectively.

Podcasting isn't just a content channel; it's a relationship-building tool that can deepen customer loyalty and drive meaningful conversations.

For listeners, this book is a celebration of podcasting's diversity and creativity. You'll gain a deeper appreciation for the medium's impact on culture, media, and technology.

You'll also learn how to discover new shows, support your favorite creators, and even leave reviews that help podcasts thrive.

A Medium for the Future

Podcasting isn't just a medium of the moment; it's a medium of the future. As technology continues to evolve, podcasts are becoming more accessible and immersive. Innovations like smart speakers, AI-driven content curation, and video podcasting are reshaping how we create and consume audio content.

Meanwhile, the growing popularity of localized and regional podcasts ensures that podcasting remains a truly global phenomenon.

The future of podcasting is bright, but it's also ripe with challenges. Issues like content saturation, discoverability, and platform consolidation pose significant hurdles for creators and listeners alike. However, these challenges also present opportunities for innovation.

By embracing creativity, authenticity, and adaptability, podcasting will continue to thrive as a space for storytelling, education, and connection.

Your Podcasting Journey Starts Here

Podcasting is more than a medium; it's a movement. It's a platform where anyone can share their voice, connect with others, and make an impact. Whether you dream of starting your own podcast, leveraging the medium for your brand, or simply exploring its rich content library, this book is your guide to understanding and embracing podcasting in all its forms.

So, let's dive in. Together, we'll explore the past, present, and future of podcasting, uncovering what makes it one of the most exciting and transformative mediums of our time. Your podcasting journey begins now.

Chapter 1

How it all began: Podcast Origins

Chapter 1 | **Origins**

Podcasting, now a booming global industry, had humble beginnings rooted in technological innovation and a desire for on-demand content.

What began as an experiment by tech enthusiasts has grown into a major medium for storytelling, education, and entertainment. Understanding the origins of podcasting reveals how the medium evolved to meet changing audience needs and cultural shifts.

Early Foundations: The Birth of Digital Audio

The seeds of podcasting were planted long before the term "podcast" was coined. In the late 1980s and 1990s, advancements in audio compression technology, such as the MP3 format, made it possible to store and share digital audio files.

The creation of the MP3 format by the Fraunhofer Society in 1993 allowed audio to be compressed into smaller file sizes without significant loss of quality, enabling easier distribution.

Simultaneously, the rise of the internet opened new avenues for sharing media. Websites and forums became hubs for distributing MP3 files, paving the way for audio-based content to be shared globally.

However, there were limitations—manual downloading and lack of automation meant the process was cumbersome for users.

The Dawn of RSS Feeds

A major breakthrough came with the introduction of RSS (Really Simple Syndication) feeds. In the late 1990s, Dave Winer, a software developer and key figure in the podcasting world, developed the RSS 2.0 specification.

This technology allowed content creators to distribute updates to their subscribers automatically. Winer's innovation became the backbone of podcasting by enabling automatic delivery of new audio episodes directly to users.

The integration of audio files into RSS feeds was pioneered by journalist and software developer Adam Curry. In 2004, Curry, often referred to as the "Podfather," created a program called iPodder, which allowed users to download internet radio broadcasts to their iPods. This innovation bridged the gap between digital audio and portable devices, making it easier for listeners to access content on the go.

Coining of "Podcast"

The term "podcast" was coined in 2004 by Ben Hammersley, a journalist writing for *The Guardian*. In an article about the rise of amateur audio blogging, Hammersley combined the words "iPod" (Apple's popular portable media player) and "broadcast."

Despite the name's association with Apple, podcasts were not exclusive to iPods and could be played on any device capable of handling MP3 files.

As podcasts gained traction, Curry and Winer collaborated to further refine the process of podcast distribution.

Their efforts laid the groundwork for what would soon become a booming industry.

The Role of Apple and iTunes

Apple played a pivotal role in popularizing podcasts. In 2005, the company added a podcast directory to its iTunes platform, providing a centralized hub for discovering and subscribing to podcasts.

This move brought podcasts into the mainstream, introducing the medium to millions of iPod users worldwide.

Apple's integration of podcasts into iTunes also established the subscription model as the standard for podcast consumption. Users could subscribe to their favorite shows, and new episodes would automatically download to their devices. This seamless experience removed many of the technical barriers that had previously limited podcast adoption.

Early Content Creators and Pioneers

The early days of podcasting saw a mix of amateur enthusiasts and professional broadcasters experimenting with the medium. Shows like *The Daily Source Code,* hosted by Adam Curry, and *This Week in Tech* (TWiT), hosted by Leo Laporte, attracted niche audiences and demonstrated the potential of podcasts to build dedicated communities.

Traditional media outlets also began to take notice. NPR (National Public Radio) in the United States was one of the first major broadcasters to embrace podcasting, repurposing its radio shows for on-demand listening.

This move helped legitimize podcasts as a credible form of media and introduced them to a broader audience.

Everybody's a Content Creator These Days

One of the defining features of podcasting is its low barrier to entry. Unlike traditional broadcasting, which requires significant financial and technical resources, podcasting allows anyone with a microphone and internet connection to create and distribute content.

This democratization has given rise to a diverse range of voices and perspectives, fueling the medium's growth.

Early platforms like Libsyn (founded in 2004) and Podbean provided hosting services specifically for podcasts, making it easier for creators to publish and distribute their content. These platforms also offered analytics tools, helping podcasters understand their audiences and refine their strategies.

Podcasting's Growth and Evolution

The late 2000s and early 2010s marked a period of steady growth for podcasting. Advances in smartphone technology, particularly the introduction of Apple's iPhone in 2007, made podcasts more accessible than ever. Dedicated podcast apps, such as Apple Podcasts, Stitcher, and Overcast, further simplified the listening experience.

The release of *Serial* in 2014 marked a turning point for podcasting. This true crime podcast, produced by Sarah Koenig and the team at *This American Life*, became a cultural phenomenon, attracting millions of listeners and proving that podcasts could achieve mainstream success. *Serial* also showcased the storytelling potential of podcasts, inspiring a wave of high-quality, narrative-driven content.

The Modern Podcasting Landscape

Today, podcasting is a global industry with millions of shows and episodes covering virtually every topic imaginable.

Major companies like Spotify and Amazon have invested heavily in podcasts, acquiring content creators and platforms to expand their reach.

The rise of video podcasts, live-streaming capabilities, and monetization opportunities through ads, sponsorships, and subscriptions has further expanded the medium's possibilities.

As technology continues to evolve, podcasting remains a dynamic and adaptable form of media, offering endless opportunities for creators and listeners alike.

Final Thoughts

Podcasting's journey from a niche hobby to a mainstream medium is a testament to the power of innovation and the enduring appeal of storytelling.

By combining technological advancements with creative freedom, podcasting has carved out a unique space in the media landscape, and its future looks brighter than ever.

Chapter 2

Humble Beginnings of Today's Top Podcasters

Chapter 2 | **Tough Starts for Top Podcasts**

Podcasting has become a dominant force in modern media, with millions of shows and billions of listeners worldwide.

Among these, a few podcasts rise to the top, captivating audiences and setting benchmarks for success. What makes these shows so popular among listeners?

Often, it's the story of their humble beginnings—a mix of passion, persistence, and creativity that catapulted them into the limelight.

Here, we'll look at the origins of five of the top podcasts dominating Apple iTunes as of January 2025, highlighting the data metrics, anecdotes from the show, and big milestones that brought them to prominence.

1. The Joe Rogan Experience

Origin Story: What started as a casual side project in 2009 has grown into one of the most influential podcasts in the world. Joe Rogan, a stand-up comedian and UFC commentator, began recording episodes with friends using basic equipment in his home studio. Initially, the show featured unfiltered conversations about comedy, fitness, and conspiracy theories.

Key Milestones: By 2020, The Joe Rogan Experience had garnered such a massive following that Spotify signed an exclusive licensing deal reportedly worth $100 million. The show regularly reaches millions of listeners per episode and has been downloaded over 11 billion times.

Host Quote: "I never thought this would become what it is today. It's proof that if you do what you love, people will connect with your authenticity," Rogan said in a 2021 interview.

2. Crime Junkie

Origin Story: Hosted by Ashley Flowers and Brit Prawat, Crime Junkie began in 2017 as a passion project fueled by Flowers' love for true crime. Flowers started by researching and scripting episodes in her free time while working a full-time job. The duo recorded their first episodes using a laptop and a basic microphone.

Key Milestones: Within a year, the podcast had skyrocketed to the top of the true crime category, thanks to its compelling storytelling and meticulous research. Crime Junkie now has over 500 million downloads, with 5 million listeners tuning in weekly.

Host Quote: "I never imagined two girls from Indiana could create something that resonates with so many people worldwide," Flowers shared in a 2023 Forbes profile.

3. Call Her Daddy

Origin Story: Alexandra Cooper and Sofia Franklyn launched Call Her Daddy in 2018, blending humor, candid relationship advice, and personal anecdotes. The pair started by recording episodes in their New York apartment, relying on social media to promote their content.

Key Milestones: The show gained viral traction, eventually securing a deal with Barstool Sports. In 2021, Cooper signed a $60 million exclusive deal with Spotify, cementing *Call Her Daddy* as one of the highest-earning podcasts globally.

Host Quote: "It's all about creating conversations people want to have but are too afraid to start," Cooper said in an interview with *The New York Times*.

4. The Daily

Origin Story: Launched by *The New York Times* in 2017, The Daily aimed to distill complex news stories into digestible, 20-minute episodes. Hosted by Michael Barbaro, the show started with a small production team and a clear mission to create engaging, narrative-driven journalism.

Key Milestones: The Daily now boasts over 4 million daily listeners and has been downloaded more than 2 billion times. It has won multiple awards, including a Webby for Best News Podcast.

Host Quote: "The idea was simple: bring listeners closer to the stories that shape our world. We didn't expect the audience to grow so rapidly," Barbaro said during a 2022 podcast convention.

5. Armchair Expert

Origin Story: Actor Dax Shepard and co-host Monica Padman launched Armchair Expert in 2018 as a space for candid conversations about life's challenges. Shepard recorded the first episodes in his attic, using minimal equipment and relying on his celebrity connections to book guests.

Key Milestones: Armchair Expert quickly climbed the charts, thanks to its raw, heartfelt interviews with high-profile guests like Kristen Bell and Barack Obama. By 2021, the podcast had partnered with Spotify in an exclusive deal.

Host Quote: "We wanted to create a show that feels like a safe space—where vulnerability and humor intersect," Shepard shared in a 2023 interview with Variety.

Common Themes in Their Success

While each of these podcasts has a unique origin story, their paths to success share common themes:

Authenticity: Whether it's Joe Rogan's candid conversations or Crime Junkie's heartfelt storytelling, authenticity resonates deeply with listeners.

Consistency: All five podcasts maintained a regular release schedule, building audience trust and loyalty over time.

Community Engagement: From social media promotions to interactive Q&A sessions, these shows fostered strong connections with their audiences.

Strategic Partnerships: Collaborations with platforms like Spotify and Barstool Sports amplified their reach and financial success.

Final Thoughts

The journey from humble beginnings to global recognition is a testament to the power of passion, persistence, and innovation. These stories prove that successful podcasting isn't about having the perfect start—it's about staying committed to delivering value to your audience.

Whether you're an aspiring podcaster or a seasoned producer, the stories of these top shows serve as inspiration to chase your vision and create something extraordinary.

Chapter 3

Did Podcasting Kill the Radio Star?

Chapter 3 | Podcasting Kill the Radio Star?

The iconic Buggles song *"Video Killed the Radio Star"* famously ushered in the MTV era, signaling a shift in media consumption.

Decades later, another question looms: did podcasting kill the radio star?

As podcasts grow in popularity, with millions of shows available at the tap of a finger, it's tempting to think that traditional radio is on its way out. But the relationship between podcasts and radio is more complex than one replacing the other.

Let's dive into the rise of podcasting, its impact on radio, and what the future holds for both mediums.

The Rise of Podcasting

Podcasting has grown exponentially in the past decade, transitioning from a niche hobby to a mainstream medium. According to Edison Research's *Infinite Dial* report, as of 2023, 64% of Americans aged 12 and older had listened to a podcast, with 42% tuning in monthly.

Globally, the podcast industry is expected to surpass $4 billion in revenue by 2024. The flexibility of on-demand audio content has attracted listeners who want to consume media on their own schedules, not dictated by radio programming.

Podcasts cover every imaginable topic, from comedy and politics to true crime and niche hobbies, providing a level of diversity that traditional radio often struggles to match. Platforms like Spotify, Apple Podcasts, and Google Podcasts have democratized access, making it easy for creators to publish content and for listeners to discover it.

The Evolution of Radio

While podcasting surges forward, traditional radio has been holding its ground in many respects.

According to Nielsen, terrestrial radio still reaches 92% of Americans weekly as of 2023, making it one of the most widely consumed media formats in the country. In-car listening remains a stronghold for radio, with commuters tuning in to music, news, and talk shows during their daily drives.

Radio's strength lies in its local presence. Unlike podcasts, which are often global in reach, local radio stations provide community news, weather updates, and traffic reports that are immediately relevant to their listeners.

Additionally, radio excels in live coverage of events, from sports games to breaking news, areas where podcasts cannot compete due to their pre-recorded nature.

Podcasting vs. Radio: Key Differences

1. **On-Demand vs. Scheduled Listening**
   Podcasts are available anytime, anywhere, giving listeners complete control over their consumption. Radio, on the other hand, relies on a fixed schedule, which can be inconvenient for today's busy audiences.

2. **Advertising Models**
   Radio relies on traditional commercials, often perceived as intrusive by listeners. Podcasts have adopted a more integrated approach with host-read ads that feel personal and authentic, leading to higher engagement rates.

3. **Content Variety**
   While radio stations are limited by their formats (Top 40, talk radio, classic rock), podcasts can delve into hyper-specific niches, attracting dedicated audiences.

4. **Cost of Entry**
   Starting a radio station requires significant capital, FCC licensing, and technical expertise. Podcasting, however, has a low barrier to entry,

with creators needing only a microphone and hosting platform to get started.

How Podcasting Challenges Radio

Podcasting's growth has undeniably challenged traditional radio. Many advertisers have shifted their budgets to podcasts, drawn by the medium's ability to target specific demographics and measure results more effectively.

For example, a study by Edison Research found that podcast ads have a 54% higher brand recall rate than traditional radio ads.

Younger audiences are also gravitating toward podcasts. A 2022 Pew Research study revealed that 60% of 18-34-year-olds in the U.S. regularly listen to podcasts, compared to 38% who tune into AM/FM radio.

This generational shift indicates that as older radio listeners age out, younger audiences may not take their place.

Moreover, the technological shift toward streaming platforms like Spotify and Pandora, which combine music playlists with podcast offerings, has further eroded radio's dominance in the audio space.

Why Radio Isn't Dead

Despite these challenges, radio remains resilient. One of radio's strengths is its adaptability. Many traditional radio broadcasters have embraced podcasting as a complementary medium rather than a competitor. NPR, for example, has become a podcasting powerhouse while maintaining its radio legacy.

Shows like *The Daily* by The New York Times and *TED Radio Hour* straddle the line between radio and podcast formats, proving that the two mediums can coexist.

Local radio also retains a unique cultural relevance. During natural disasters or emergencies, radio often becomes a lifeline for communities, offering real-time updates that podcasts cannot match.

The Hybrid Future of Audio Media

The relationship between podcasts and radio may not be a zero-sum game. Instead, the two mediums seem to be evolving toward a hybrid future.

Many radio stations now offer on-demand versions of their shows as podcasts, ensuring they remain accessible to digital-first audiences.

Similarly, podcasts are experimenting with live formats and streaming capabilities, blurring the line between the two platforms.

Platforms like Clubhouse and Spotify's Greenroom have introduced live, interactive audio formats that combine the spontaneity of radio with the intimacy of podcasting.

Inspiration from Radio Stars Turned Podcasters

Many traditional radio hosts have successfully transitioned to podcasting, proving that the skills honed in radio can translate to success in the podcasting world. For instance:

- **Howard Stern**: The "king of all media" revolutionized talk radio and has adapted his format to SiriusXM, incorporating podcast-style features.
- **Dan Patrick**: The sports radio legend expanded his reach with *The Dan Patrick Show*, available as both a live radio broadcast and podcast.
- **Terry Gross**: Her iconic NPR show *Fresh Air* is one of the most downloaded podcasts,

demonstrating that quality content transcends medium boundaries.

Radio vs. Podcasting: Did We Just Become Best Friends?

So, did podcasting kill the radio star? The answer is no—but it did change the game. Podcasting has diversified the audio landscape, creating opportunities for new voices and niche content. However, radio's deep-rooted presence and ability to adapt ensure it remains relevant in the digital age.

Rather than viewing podcasting and radio as adversaries, it's more accurate to see them as complementary mediums, each with its strengths. As technology continues to evolve, the lines between the two will likely blur further, creating a richer, more dynamic audio ecosystem for creators and listeners alike.

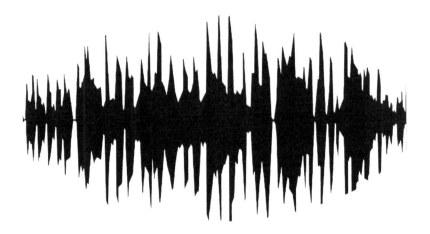

CASE STUDY

Finding Your Niche

Chapter 4

The Rise of *Spittin' Chiclets*: How a Hockey Podcast Scored a Loyal Fanbase

Case Study | Spittin' Chiclets

In the ever-expanding universe of sports podcasts, *Spittin' Chiclets* has carved out a unique and undeniable niche.

What began as a casual, hockey-centric chat in 2016 has grown into one of the most popular sports podcasts in the world, blending humor, insider stories, and a love for the game.

With a rabid fanbase, lucrative partnerships, and consistent chart-topping success, the podcast has become a cultural phenomenon, especially among hockey fans. So how did *Spittin' Chiclets* rise to such prominence, and what makes it resonate so deeply with its listeners?

The Genesis of *Spittin' Chiclets*

The podcast was born when Barstool Sports partnered with retired NHL player **Ryan Whitney** and journalist **Brian "Rear Admiral" McGonagle**.

Initially, the show's format was simple: a couple of guys talking about hockey. Whitney's charismatic personality, coupled with McGonagle's sharp wit and deep knowledge of the sport, quickly attracted listeners. Soon after, **Paul Bissonnette**, known as "Biz Nasty," joined the team, injecting even more humor and relatability into the mix.

Bissonnette later described the early days of the show as "pure chaos."

"We had no script, no real plan. It was just a few guys shooting the breeze about hockey and life," he said in a 2021 interview with *Sportsnet*.

Yet, it was precisely this unscripted, authentic dynamic that resonated with listeners.

By 2018, *Spittin' Chiclets* was a full-fledged phenomenon, boasting millions of downloads per episode and topping podcast charts worldwide.

Humor, Authenticity, and Locker Room Stories

One of the key ingredients in *Spittin' Chiclets'* success is its humor. The hosts—all former hockey players or hockey die-hards—share stories that feel like they've been plucked straight out of a locker room.

Whether it's Whitney poking fun at his own NHL career or Bissonnette recounting absurd tales from his playing days, the show strikes a perfect balance between comedy and insider insight.

"We're not trying to be the most polished sports analysts," Whitney said in an interview with *The Athletic*. "We're just telling stories and having a good time. That's what people love about it - it's real."

Listeners often cite the hosts' candor and humor as reasons for their loyalty. Unlike traditional sports media, *Spittin' Chiclets* isn't afraid to delve into the lighter, sometimes ridiculous side of hockey culture. From pranks to locker room antics, the podcast offers a glimpse into a world that fans rarely get to see.

A Platform for Players' Voices

Another unique aspect of *Spittin' Chiclets* is its guest roster. The podcast regularly features current and former NHL players, coaches, and personalities. These guests often share stories that wouldn't make it to traditional media outlets, offering a more personal and unfiltered perspective.

For example, in a 2020 episode, Sidney Crosby opened up about his pre-game rituals and his thoughts on the evolution of hockey, something fans seldom hear in press conferences.

"It's like a therapy session," Crosby joked during the episode. "You guys make it easy to talk about stuff we usually keep to ourselves."

The podcast's ability to foster such candid conversations has made it a favorite among players as well as fans.

As Bissonnette noted, "Guys trust us because we've been in their shoes. We're not here to spin headlines; we just want to tell their stories."

The Numbers Behind the Success

The metrics behind *Spittin' Chiclets*' success are nothing short of impressive. As of 2023, the podcast averages over 500,000 downloads per episode, making it one of the most popular sports podcasts globally.

It consistently ranks in the top five on Apple Podcasts' sports charts and has a significant presence on Spotify as well.

Social media engagement is another key indicator of the show's popularity. The podcast's X and Instagram accounts boast millions of followers, and fans often interact with the hosts and each other, creating a vibrant online community.

Memes, clips, and inside jokes from the show frequently go viral, further solidifying its cultural impact.

Then there's the merchandise. The *Spittin' Chiclets* brand, which includes apparel and their wildly successful Pink Whitney vodka (a collaboration with New Amsterdam Vodka), generates millions in annual revenue.

Pink Whitney alone reportedly sold over a million cases in its first year, a testament to the podcast's ability to mobilize its fanbase.

Relatability: The Heart of the Podcast

What truly sets *Spittin' Chiclets* apart is its relatability. While the hosts bring insider knowledge and access to the table, they never come across as untouchable experts.

Instead, they feel like friends you'd want to grab a beer with.

This accessibility has endeared them to fans across the hockey spectrum—from die-hard enthusiasts to casual viewers.

In a 2022 interview with *ESPN*, Rear Admiral summed it up perfectly: "We're just regular guys who love hockey. And that's why people connect with us. We're not trying to be something we're not."

Tackling Serious Issues

While *Spittin' Chiclets* is known for its humor, the podcast isn't afraid to tackle serious topics. Episodes have addressed issues like mental health, substance abuse, and the pressures of professional sports.

The hosts' willingness to share their own struggles has made these discussions especially impactful.

"We've all been through our own battles," Bissonnette said during a 2021 episode. "If talking about it helps even one person, it's worth it."

These moments of vulnerability add depth to the show and highlight its broader cultural significance. It's not just about hockey; it's about life, resilience, and finding humor even in the toughest situations.

The Future of *Spittin' Chiclets*

As *Spittin' Chiclets* continues to grow, its influence shows no signs of waning. The hosts have hinted at expanding into live events, documentaries, and even more branded products.

Their ability to innovate while staying true to their roots suggests that the podcast will remain a dominant force in sports media for years to come.

"We're just getting started," Whitney said in a recent episode. "The Daddy Gang has Pink Whitney; now it's time for the Chiclets crew to take over the world."

Final Thoughts ...

The rise of *Spittin' Chiclets* is a testament to the power of authenticity, humor, and a deep love for the game of hockey. By offering fans a unique blend of insider stories, unfiltered commentary, and genuine camaraderie, the podcast has become more than just a show—it's a community.

As the hosts would say, it's not just about spittin' chiclets; it's about building something bigger. And with millions of listeners tuning in every week, it's safe to say they've succeeded.

Chapter 5

The Role of Podcasting in the 2024 Presidential Campaign

Chapter 5 | **Podcasting Elections**

In the 2024 U.S. Presidential election podcasting emerged as a pivotal medium that significantly influenced voter sentiment, particularly benefiting Donald Trump's campaign.

The strategic utilization of podcasts allowed Trump to connect with diverse audiences, especially younger demographics, in a manner that traditional media channels could not match.

Podcasting has experienced exponential growth in recent years. As of 2024, over 100 million Americans were regular podcast listeners, with a significant portion aged between 18 and 34. This demographic alignment presented a unique opportunity for political campaigns to engage with younger voters through a medium they trust and regularly consume.

Trump's Strategic Podcast Appearances

Donald Trump's campaign capitalized on the podcasting boom by scheduling appearances on several high-profile shows. Notably, his interviews on "The Joe Rogan Experience," "PBD Podcast," and "Impaulsive" garnered millions of views and listens, amplifying his reach beyond traditional news outlets.

These platforms provided unfiltered environments where Trump could articulate his policies and personality without the constraints typical of mainstream media.

Impact on Voter Demographics

Data indicates that Trump's podcast appearances resonated particularly well with younger male voters.

According to exit polls, there was a noticeable shift in support among males aged 18 to 29, with a 5% increase in votes for Trump compared to the 2020 election. This demographic, which consumes podcasts at higher rates, was directly targeted through his strategic media engagements.

The Joe Rogan Effect

One of the most influential platforms was "The Joe Rogan Experience," which boasts an estimated 11 million listeners per episode. Rogan's endorsement and subsequent interview with Trump provided access to a vast, predominantly young male audience. Analysts suggest that this appearance played a crucial role in swaying undecided voters within this group.

Comparative Analysis with Opponent's Media Strategy

In contrast, Democratic nominee Kamala Harris's campaign was less active in the podcasting arena. While Harris did make some appearances, they did not achieve the same level of engagement or reach.

This disparity in media strategy is highlighted by the fact that Trump's podcast interviews collectively amassed over 50 million views and listens, whereas Harris's engagements garnered significantly fewer.

The Role of Alternative Media

The 2024 election underscored the growing influence of alternative media ecosystems. Conservative podcasters and influencers created a parallel media landscape that effectively mobilized and informed their audiences.

This network's ability to disseminate campaign messages and counter mainstream narratives provided Trump with a substantial advantage.

Statistical Correlations

A study by the Pew Research Center found that 60% of podcast listeners reported being influenced by the content they consumed.

Furthermore, among regular listeners of political podcasts, there was a 70% likelihood of voting for the candidate featured most frequently in their preferred shows. These statistics underscore the persuasive power of podcasting as a medium.

Final Thoughts

The 2024 U.S. Presidential election highlighted the transformative impact of podcasting in political campaigns. Donald Trump's strategic engagement with this medium enabled him to connect with key voter demographics, disseminate his message unfiltered, and ultimately secure electoral success.

As podcasting continues to grow, its role in shaping political landscapes will undoubtedly become even more pronounced.

Chapter 6

Key Metrics for Podcasts:

What They Are and Why They Matter

Chapter 6 | **Key Metrics**

The podcasting industry continues to grow at an astonishing rate, with millions of shows vying for listener attention. Whether you're an independent creator or part of a larger media organization, understanding key podcast metrics is essential to evaluate performance, refine your content strategy, and attract sponsors.

But what do these metrics mean, and how can they guide your podcast's growth? Here's a detailed breakdown of the most important podcast metrics and what they reveal about your show.

1. Downloads and Streams

One of the most widely tracked metrics in podcasting, downloads and streams represent the number of times an episode is accessed by listeners. A download occurs when someone saves your episode to their device, while a stream involves listening directly without downloading.

Why It Matters: Downloads and streams offer a basic indication of your podcast's reach. However, they don't necessarily mean someone listened to the entire episode. For a more accurate understanding of listener engagement, you'll need to look at additional metrics.

2. Listeners

Listeners refer to the number of unique individuals who tune into your podcast. Unlike downloads, this metric accounts for duplicate listens, offering a more accurate count of your audience size.

Why It Matters: Tracking unique listeners helps you understand how many people your content is truly reaching. It's especially valuable when you're trying to demonstrate audience size to potential sponsors or partners.

3. Audience Demographics

Demographic data includes information about your listeners, such as their age, gender, location, and interests. This information is often collected by podcast hosting platforms or streaming services.

Why It Matters: Knowing your audience demographics allows you to tailor your content and marketing strategies. For example, if most of your listeners are in their 20s and based in urban areas, you can create topics or campaigns that resonate with their experiences and preferences.

4. Engagement Metrics

Engagement metrics track how listeners interact with your podcast. Key indicators include:
- **Completion Rate:** The percentage of an episode that listeners consume.

- **Average Listening Time:** How long listeners stay tuned before dropping off.
- **Listener Retention:** The percentage of returning listeners versus first-time listeners.

Why It Matters: High engagement metrics signal that your content is resonating with your audience. If listeners consistently drop off midway through episodes, it may be a sign to reevaluate your pacing, structure, or content.

5. Subscriptions or Follows

This metric tracks the number of people who have subscribed to or followed your podcast on platforms like Spotify, Apple Podcasts, or Google Podcasts.

Why It Matters: Subscriptions indicate sustained interest in your content. A growing number of followers suggests that your podcast is building a loyal audience. Many platforms prioritize shows with higher subscription rates, making this metric crucial for discoverability.

6. Reviews and Ratings

Reviews and ratings are public feedback from your audience, often available on podcast directories like Apple Podcasts.

Why It Matters: Positive reviews and high ratings can boost your podcast's credibility and visibility. They also provide social proof to potential listeners, encouraging them to give your show a try.

While reviews are subjective, they often offer valuable insights into what your audience enjoys or dislikes about your content.

7. Social Media Engagement

Social media metrics track how your audience interacts with your podcast's content on platforms like

Instagram, X, or TikTok. These interactions include likes, shares, comments, and mentions.

Why It Matters: Social media engagement is an indirect but important indicator of your podcast's popularity and reach. It also helps you connect with your audience in real-time, fostering community and loyalty. Viral social media moments can even attract new listeners to your show.

8. Website Traffic

If you host your podcast on a dedicated website, tracking website traffic is essential. Metrics to monitor include page views, unique visitors, and the average time spent on your site.

Why It Matters: Your website serves as a hub for your podcast, offering additional content like show notes, merchandise, or bonus episodes. High website traffic suggests that your audience values these resources and considers your podcast a reliable brand.

9. Ad Performance Metrics

For podcasters monetizing their shows, ad performance metrics are critical. These include:

- **CPM (Cost Per Mille):** Earnings per 1,000 downloads.
- **CTR (Click-Through Rate):** The percentage of listeners who engage with your call-to-action or sponsor link.

Why It Matters: Strong ad performance metrics demonstrate the effectiveness of your podcast as a marketing channel. This data is crucial when negotiating sponsorship deals or pricing ad spots.

10. Podcast Ranking

Many podcast platforms feature rankings or charts that list the most popular shows in various categories.

Why It Matters: A high ranking boosts your podcast's visibility, attracting more listeners and advertisers. While rankings can fluctuate, consistently appearing in charts can establish your podcast as a leader in its niche.

11. Listener Growth Rate

This metric tracks how quickly your audience is expanding over time. It's calculated by comparing listener numbers across different time periods.

Why It Matters: A steady growth rate indicates that your marketing strategies and content are working. Sharp declines, on the other hand, may signal the need for adjustments.

12. Episode-Specific Performance

Evaluating individual episodes helps you identify which topics, formats, or guests resonate most with your audience. Key metrics include downloads, completion rates, and engagement levels for specific episodes.

Why It Matters: Episode-specific analysis allows you to replicate successes and learn from underperforming content. It's a valuable tool for refining your editorial strategy.

Final Thoughts

Understanding and tracking podcast metrics isn't just about numbers—it's about gaining insights into your audience and the impact of your content. By focusing on these key metrics, you can make data-driven decisions to improve your podcast, grow your audience, and achieve your goals.

Remember, every podcast is unique, so the metrics that matter most will depend on your objectives and the audience you aim to serve.

Chapter 7

How Successful Podcasts Make Money: A Data-Driven Guide

Chapter 7 | Monetization 101

Podcasting has evolved from a niche medium into a booming industry. As of 2023, there are over 5 million podcasts globally, with 464.7 million listeners, according to Statista.

With this explosive growth, podcasts are no longer just passion projects; they've become a lucrative avenue for creators and businesses alike.

But how do successful podcasts generate revenue? This article delves into the key monetization strategies employed by top podcasters, backed by statistical data and insights from reputable networks.

1. Sponsorships and Advertising: The Backbone of Podcast Revenue

Sponsorships and advertising are the most common and lucrative sources of income for podcasters.

Advertisers are drawn to the medium because of its highly engaged and niche audiences.

According to a report by the Interactive Advertising Bureau (IAB) and PricewaterhouseCoopers (PwC), podcast advertising revenue reached $2.2 billion in 2023 and is projected to surpass $4 billion by 2025.

How It Works:

Podcasters include ads within their episodes, either as pre-roll (before the content), mid-roll (during the content), or post-roll (after the content). These ads can be dynamically inserted based on listener demographics or host-read for a more personal touch.

Key Statistic: Podcasters typically earn $18 to $50 per 1,000 listens (CPM) for host-read ads, depending on the niche and audience loyalty. For example, a podcast with 50,000 monthly downloads can generate $900 to $2,500 per month from ads alone.

Success Story: The podcast The Joe Rogan Experience, before its exclusive Spotify deal, earned an estimated $30 million annually from ads and sponsorships, according to Forbes.

2. Listener Donations and Crowdfunding: Building Community Support

Listener donations provide an opportunity for fans to directly support their favorite podcasts. Platforms like Patreon, Buy Me a Coffee, and Kickstarter enable podcasters to offer exclusive content or perks in exchange for financial contributions.

How It Works:
Podcasters create tiered memberships where listeners can access bonus episodes, early content, or merchandise. This strategy works best for shows with a dedicated fanbase.

Key Statistic: Patreon reports that creators in its "Audio" category, which includes podcasters, earn an average of $2,000 per month. High-performing podcasts can earn significantly more; for example, "Chapo Trap House" earns over $180,000 monthly from Patreon subscribers.

Success Story: "Last Podcast on the Left," a comedy-horror podcast, generates significant revenue through Patreon, boasting over 14,000 subscribers as of 2023.

3. Merchandise Sales: Extending the Brand

Merchandise is another effective way for podcasters to monetize their content. By selling branded products such as T-shirts, mugs, or stickers, podcasters can capitalize on their loyal listeners while strengthening their brand identity.

How It Works:
Merchandise is often sold through e-commerce platforms like Shopify or integrated into crowdfunding campaigns. Popular podcasts often create

limited-edition items to create a sense of urgency among fans.

Key Statistic: According to Printful, profit margins for custom merchandise typically range from 20% to 50%. A podcast with a strong following can generate thousands of dollars monthly from merchandise alone.

Success Story: "My Favorite Murder," a true crime podcast, has built a multimillion-dollar brand that includes merchandise sales. Their "Murderino" fanbase is known for purchasing everything from apparel to custom tote bags.

4. Subscription Models and Paywalled Content

With the rise of platforms like Apple Podcasts Subscriptions and Spotify's paid podcasting feature, subscription-based models have become a significant revenue stream. Podcasters can charge listeners a monthly fee for exclusive or ad-free content.

How It Works:

Listeners pay a recurring fee (usually between $3 to $10 per month) for access to premium episodes, behind-the-scenes content, or early releases.

Key Statistic: A 2022 survey by Supercast revealed that podcasters with paid subscription models earn an average of $7 per subscriber per month. Even small shows with 500 paying subscribers can generate $3,500 monthly.

Success Story: "Call Her Daddy," a popular podcast now exclusive to Spotify, used subscription-based content to build a dedicated audience before securing a $60 million licensing deal.

5. Affiliate Marketing: Leveraging Listener Trust

Affiliate marketing involves podcasters promoting products or services and earning a commission for each sale made through their unique referral links.

How It Works:

Podcasters recommend products that align with their content and audience. Links are shared in show notes, websites, or social media posts, and creators earn a percentage of the revenue from purchases.

Key Statistic: Affiliate commission rates range from 5% to 30% per sale, depending on the program. According to HubSpot, podcasts with niche audiences can achieve conversion rates as high as 8%.

Success Story: Tech-focused podcasts often excel in affiliate marketing. "The Vergecast," for example, earns significant revenue by promoting gadgets and software to its tech-savvy listeners.

6. Licensing and Syndication Deals: Scaling the Brand

Successful podcasts often strike licensing or syndication deals with major platforms or media companies. These agreements involve granting rights to distribute or adapt podcast content for a fixed fee or percentage of revenue.

How It Works:
Licensing deals are typically offered to podcasts with large audiences or unique content. Syndication involves redistributing podcast episodes across multiple platforms.

Key Statistic: Licensing deals can range from $10,000 to multi-million-dollar contracts. Spotify alone invested over $1 billion in podcast acquisitions and licensing deals between 2019 and 2023.

Success Story: "The Daily," produced by The New York Times, has extended its brand through syndication agreements with radio stations, generating significant revenue.

7. Live Shows/Events: Engaging Fans in Real Life

Live events offer podcasters an opportunity to monetize their audience through ticket sales, merchandise, and sponsorships. These events often include live recordings, meet-and-greets, or panel discussions.

How It Works:
Podcasters partner with event venues or participate in podcast festivals to host live shows. Ticket prices typically range from $20 to $50.

Key Statistic: Eventbrite data shows that small-scale podcast events can generate between $5,000 and $20,000 per show, depending on audience size and venue capacity.

Success Story: "Welcome to Night Vale," a fictional storytelling podcast, has successfully toured internationally, selling out venues and generating substantial revenue.

8. Grants and Public Funding: Nonprofit Models

Educational and nonprofit podcasts can secure funding through grants or public donations. Organizations like the Knight Foundation and Google Podcasts creator program offer financial support to creators who focus on public service content.

How It Works:
Podcasters apply for grants with detailed proposals and budgets. Public funding can also be obtained through listener contributions on platforms like Kickstarter.

Key Statistic: Grant amounts range from $5,000 to $50,000, depending on the scope and purpose of the project.

Success Story: "Science Vs," a podcast debunking scientific myths, received funding from multiple organizations to continue producing high-quality content.

Final Thoughts

Successful podcasts employ a mix of revenue streams tailored to their audience and content. Whether through advertising, listener support, merchandise, or licensing deals, the possibilities for monetization are vast.

By leveraging analytics and audience insights, podcasters can identify the most effective strategies to ensure financial sustainability and long-term growth.

As the podcasting industry continues to expand, creators who embrace diverse revenue models are best positioned to thrive.

Chapter 8

Megyn Kelly: From Network News to Star Podcast Interviewer

CASE STUDY | A **Masterclass in Interviewing**

Megyn Kelly is no stranger to the limelight. As a former network news anchor for Fox News and later NBC, Kelly commanded the airwaves for years, delivering hard-hitting interviews and hosting primetime specials.

Yet, her transition from network television to the world of podcasting was as surprising as it was transformative. *The Megyn Kelly Show*, which debuted in 2020, has rapidly risen to prominence as one of the most popular political and cultural commentary podcasts.

With its mix of sharp analysis, engaging interviews, and Kelly's signature no-nonsense style, the show has resonated deeply with fans across the nation.

A Bold Transition

When Megyn Kelly announced her departure from NBC in 2019, many wondered what her next move would be. Transitioning from a network news career that had defined her for over a decade to the comparatively niche world of podcasting was a gamble.

Reflecting on her journey, Kelly stated, "It was liberating. I didn't want to be confined by corporate agendas anymore. Podcasting gave me the freedom to be myself, to explore topics I care about deeply, and to speak directly to my audience without filters."

This willingness to step away from traditional media's safety net turned out to be a smart move. In her podcast, Kelly's authenticity shines through, a quality that many listeners felt was diminished during her network years.

Fans often say the podcast feels like a conversation with an old friend—someone unafraid to tackle controversial subjects while remaining grounded.

The Ingredients of Success

So, what makes *The Megyn Kelly Show* resonate so profoundly with its audience? Part of its appeal lies in its versatility. The podcast covers a wide range of topics, from breaking political news to societal trends and personal stories.

Kelly's background as a journalist allows her to conduct incisive interviews with a wide variety of guests, ranging from politicians and cultural critics to comedians and thought leaders.

As Kelly herself puts it, "The best conversations happen when you're willing to listen, even if you don't agree. My podcast is about honest dialogue, not echo chambers."

This approach has drawn praise from both fans and critics. A 2022 analysis by Edison Research noted that

The Megyn Kelly Show ranks among the top 1% of podcasts globally in terms of audience reach, with millions of downloads per episode. This impressive metric places it alongside industry giants like *The Joe Rogan Experience* and *The Daily.*

Metrics and Milestones

Kelly's podcast success is no accident. It's built on a foundation of meticulous production, audience engagement, and strategic marketing. The show's growth trajectory is underscored by several key metrics:

1. Audience Reach: According to Podtrac, *The Megyn Kelly Show* consistently ranks in the top 10 for news and political commentary podcasts in the United States.

2. Diverse Demographics: While many political podcasts skew heavily male or female, Kelly's audience boasts a nearly equal gender split. This balance is unusual in the podcasting world and speaks to her ability to appeal to a broad spectrum of listeners.

3. Social Media Influence: Kelly's social media presence has played a crucial role in the podcast's rise. With millions of followers across platforms, she uses her reach to promote episodes, tease content, and engage directly with her audience.

4. Revenue Streams: By leveraging a mix of sponsorships, premium subscription tiers, and merchandise sales, Kelly has turned her podcast into a lucrative enterprise. Industry insiders estimate her annual earnings from the podcast exceed $10 million.

Quotes That Define Her Journey

Kelly has often spoken candidly about her transition to podcasting. In an interview with *The Wall Street*

Journal, she remarked, "The news industry has become too polarized. I wanted to create a space where people can hear diverse opinions without shouting matches."

On the freedom podcasting affords her, Kelly told *The New York Times*: "I'm not chasing ratings. I'm chasing the truth. That's the luxury of this medium."

These statements reflect the core ethos of her show: an unvarnished commitment to exploring ideas and challenging assumptions without pandering to one side of the political spectrum.

The "Kelly Touch"

What truly sets Kelly apart in the podcasting landscape is her ability to balance hard-hitting analysis with moments of levity and humanity.

In one memorable episode, Kelly joked about how her children critique her podcasting skills, saying, "Mom, you're so much cooler on the podcast than on TV!" These glimpses into her personal life make the podcast relatable, even as it tackles weighty topics.

Listeners have also praised Kelly's willingness to admit when she's wrong—a rarity in today's polarized media environment.

During a 2023 episode discussing cancel culture, she acknowledged, "I've been part of the problem before, but I'm learning, just like everyone else." Such moments of humility resonate deeply with her audience.

A Cultural Touchstone

The success of *The Megyn Kelly Show* is emblematic of a larger trend: the rise of independent media voices in the podcasting space. In an age where trust in traditional media is declining, podcasts like Kelly's provide an alternative that feels more personal, transparent, and engaging.

As Kelly's audience continues to grow, so does her influence. A 2023 Pew Research study found that 45% of podcast listeners consider podcasts a more trustworthy source of news than traditional outlets. Kelly's success underscores this shift and highlights the growing power of the podcasting medium.

Lessons for Aspiring Podcasters

For those looking to emulate Kelly's success, several key takeaways emerge:

Authenticity Matters: Kelly's willingness to be herself—flaws and all—is a significant part of her appeal.

Diverse Content: By covering a wide range of topics, Kelly ensures her podcast remains relevant and engaging.

Audience Engagement: Kelly's active interaction with her audience fosters a sense of community that traditional media often lacks

.

High-Quality Production: Professional editing, sound quality, and strategic marketing are non-negotiable for top-tier podcasts.

Final Thoughts …

Megyn Kelly's rise in the podcasting world is a testament to the power of reinvention, authenticity, and connection. By leaving behind the constraints of network news, she's carved out a space where ideas can flourish, and listeners feel heard.

As Kelly herself puts it, "This podcast isn't just about me; it's about us. It's about having the conversations that matter."

Whether you agree with her or not, there's no denying the impact of *The Megyn Kelly Show*. It's more than a podcast; it's a cultural phenomenon that continues to shape the media landscape.

Chapter 9

Podcasting or Live stream?

Chapter 9 | **Podcast vs. Streaming**

As digital content continues to evolve, two major formats have risen to prominence—podcasting and live streaming.

Each has carved out a unique space in the media landscape, offering creators and audiences distinct advantages and challenges.

Whether you're a budding content creator or an established brand, understanding the nuances of podcasting and livestreaming can help you decide which format best aligns with your goals. Here, we'll dive deep into the pros and cons of each format, using insights from some of the most successful shows and data metrics available.

The Podcasting Boom

Advantages of Podcasting

On-Demand Convenience: One of podcasting's most significant advantages is its on-demand nature. Listeners can tune in anytime, whether during their morning commute, workout, or downtime. This flexibility has contributed to the medium's popularity, with Edison Research reporting in 2023 that 42% of Americans listen to podcasts monthly.

High Production Quality: Podcasts, especially those produced by top creators like *The Joe Rogan Experience* or *Crime Junkie*, often feature polished audio, engaging storytelling, and professional editing. This attention to quality enhances listener retention and builds a loyal audience.

Long-Form Content: Podcasts excel at delivering in-depth discussions and storytelling. With episodes often ranging from 30 minutes to over two hours, they allow creators to explore topics thoroughly, creating a deeper connection with the audience.

Evergreen Content: Unlike livestreams, podcasts remain accessible indefinitely. This longevity ensures that new listeners can discover older episodes, contributing to sustained growth and monetization opportunities over time.

Disadvantages of Podcasting

Delayed Engagement: Podcasting lacks the immediacy of live streaming. While listener feedback often comes in the form of reviews or social media comments, there's no real-time interaction.

Production Costs: High-quality podcasts require decent equipment, editing software, and potentially professional sound engineers. For beginners, this can be a significant initial investment.

Discoverability Challenges: With over 5 million podcasts available as of 2024 (Podcast Index), standing out can be difficult. Creators need to invest in marketing and SEO strategies to reach their target audience.

The Live streaming landscape

Advantages of Live Streaming

Real-Time Engagement: Live streaming thrives on immediate interaction. Platforms like X, YouTube Live, and Instagram Live allow creators to engage with their audience through comments, polls, and Q&A sessions, fostering a sense of community.

Spontaneity: Live streams often have an unfiltered and authentic feel. This rawness can be appealing to viewers who value transparency and real-time reactions.

Multi-Purpose Content: Live streams can be repurposed into other formats, such as highlight reels, short-form videos, or even podcast episodes. This versatility maximizes content value.

Lower Entry Barrier: While professional-grade equipment enhances production, many successful livestreamers start with minimal tools, such as a smartphone and a stable internet connection.

Disadvantages of Live streaming

Nature of Social: While some platforms allow creators to save and share past streams, the content often feels transient. Audiences who miss the live broadcast may not prioritize catching up.

Technical Challenges: Live streaming demands a reliable internet connection, and technical glitches can disrupt the experience. Additionally, creators need to be comfortable handling unexpected issues on the fly.

Audience Expectations: Livestream viewers often expect frequent, consistent broadcasts. This demand can lead to burnout for creators who struggle to maintain a regular schedule.

Successful Podcasts vs. Livestreams

Podcasting Success: *Serial* and *The Joe Rogan Experience*

Serial revolutionized the podcasting landscape in 2014 by delivering a compelling narrative format. Its meticulously researched episodes set a benchmark for storytelling, garnering over 300 million downloads by 2023. The show's longevity underscores podcasting's potential for evergreen content.

Meanwhile, *The Joe Rogan Experience* demonstrates the profitability of podcasting. In 2020, Spotify signed an exclusive licensing deal worth $100 million for the podcast. Its long-form, unfiltered conversations appeal to a diverse audience, showcasing the medium's scalability and revenue potential.

Live streaming Success: *Ninja* and *Hot Ones Live*

Ninja, a professional gamer and Twitch streamer, built a massive following through real-time engagement with fans. His livestreams often feature interactive gameplay and community-driven content, which have attracted sponsorship deals and brand collaborations.

Similarly, *Hot Ones Live* extended the popular YouTube series into the livestreaming space. This adaptation leveraged the immediacy of live Q&A sessions and audience participation while retaining the show's signature format of celebrity interviews over spicy wings.

Key Metrics: Podcasting vs. Live streaming

Podcasting Metrics:

Downloads and Streams: These indicate the reach and popularity of episodes.

Listener Retention: Shows how long audiences stay engaged.

Monetization Opportunities: Sponsorships, affiliate marketing, and subscription models dominate.

Live streaming Metrics:

Concurrent Viewers: Reflects the number of viewers watching live.

Chat Interaction: Measures real-time engagement.

Revenue Streams: Includes ad revenue, donations, and subscriptions.

Choosing the Right Format

Ultimately, the choice between podcasting and livestreaming depends on your goals, audience, and resources. If you prioritize high-quality, evergreen content that allows for deep dives, podcasting may be your best bet.

On the other hand, if real-time interaction and spontaneity appeal to you, live streaming offers unparalleled opportunities to connect with your audience.

Final thoughts …

Podcasting and livestreaming each bring unique strengths to the table. While podcasts offer polished, long-form content with lasting value, live streams provide immediate, interactive experiences.

By understanding the advantages and disadvantages of each format, creators can make informed decisions to maximize their impact and grow their audience.

Chapter 10

Video vs. Audio Podcasts:

Weighing the Pros and Cons

Chapter 10 | **Audio vs. Video**

Podcasting has grown exponentially in the last decade, transforming from a niche medium into a powerful tool for storytelling, education, and marketing. But with this growth comes a key decision for creators: Should you produce a video podcast, an audio podcast, or both?

Each format offers unique opportunities and challenges. Let's explore the pros and cons of both formats to help you decide which aligns with your goals and audience expectations.

Audio Podcasts: The Original Format

Audio podcasts, the traditional format of the medium, have stood the test of time. They're simple, accessible, and versatile.

Pros of Audio Podcasts

1. **Ease of Production**

   Producing an audio podcast is generally more straightforward and affordable. With just a microphone, editing software, and a quiet space, creators can produce high-quality content. This simplicity makes audio podcasts especially appealing to beginners or those on a tight budget.

2. **Accessibility and Portability**

   Audio podcasts can be consumed anywhere—while driving, exercising, cooking, or commuting. Their hands-free nature makes them ideal for multitasking, appealing to busy audiences.

3. **Lower Data Consumption**

   Streaming or downloading audio files requires significantly less data than video. This makes audio podcasts more accessible in regions with limited internet bandwidth or for listeners with data constraints.

4. **Focus on Content**

   Without visual distractions, listeners tend to

focus more on the spoken content. This can be advantageous for storytelling, interviews, or educational topics that rely heavily on narrative or detailed explanations.

5. **Broader Platform Distribution**
Audio podcasts are easily distributed across platforms like Spotify, Apple Podcasts, Google Podcasts, and Amazon Music. These platforms have millions of active users and robust discovery algorithms.

Cons of Audio Podcasts

1. **Limited Visual Engagement**
Audio lacks a visual component, which can make it harder to capture and retain the attention of viewers who prefer more dynamic, visual content.

2. **Reduced Branding Opportunities**
Visual branding elements like logos, animations, and facial expressions are absent in audio podcasts. This can limit the depth of connection between the host and audience.

3. **Challenging for Demonstrative Topics**

   Topics that require visual aids, such as tutorials, product reviews, or demonstrations, are less effective in an audio-only format.

Video Podcasts: The Visual Evolution

Video podcasts, often distributed via platforms like YouTube, Vimeo, or Twitch, have gained traction in recent years. They combine the storytelling power of audio with the engagement potential of visual media.

Pros of Video Podcasts

1. **Enhanced Engagement**

   Visual elements like facial expressions, body language, and on-screen graphics create a more immersive experience. Studies show that viewers retain more information when it is presented visually and aurally.

2. **Broader Audience Reach**

   Video podcasts tap into the vast audiences of video-first platforms like YouTube, which boasts over 2 billion monthly users. These platforms also offer powerful discovery and recommendation algorithms that can expose your podcast to new viewers.

3. **Stronger Branding Opportunities**
Video allows for the integration of branded visuals, such as custom intros, logos, and overlays. This strengthens your brand identity and makes your content more memorable.

4. **Monetization Potential**
Platforms like YouTube offer ad revenue opportunities through their Partner Program. Video content is also more attractive to sponsors, as they can incorporate visual ads or product placements.

5. **Visual Storytelling**
For creators covering topics like cooking, fitness, design, or tech, video provides the necessary medium to demonstrate concepts visually. This enhances audience understanding and satisfaction.

Cons of Video Podcasts

1. **Higher Production Costs**
   Producing video content requires more equipment, such as cameras, lighting, and editing software. This increases the initial investment and ongoing production costs.

2. **Time-Consuming Production**
   Video editing is more complex and time-intensive than audio editing. Ensuring high-quality visuals and synchronized audio demands more effort and expertise.

3. **Bandwidth and Storage Challenges**
   Video files are significantly larger than audio files, requiring more storage space and higher bandwidth for uploads and downloads. This can limit accessibility for audiences with slower internet speeds.

4. **Limited Multitasking Appeal**
   Watching a video podcast demands full attention, reducing its appeal for listeners who enjoy consuming content while multitasking.

5. **On-Camera Presence**

   Not all hosts are comfortable being on camera. Additionally, video requires attention to appearance, setting, and on-screen charisma, which may not come naturally to every podcaster.

Key Metrics and Industry Trends

The choice between video and audio podcasts can also depend on audience preferences and industry trends. Here are some statistics to consider:

- **Audience Preferences:** According to a 2023 report by Edison Research, 78% of podcast listeners consume audio-only content, while 22% prefer video. However, the popularity of video podcasts is growing, especially among younger audiences.
- **Platform Dominance:** YouTube emerged as the top platform for podcast consumption in 2024, surpassing Spotify and Apple Podcasts.

This underscores the rising demand for video content.

- **Engagement Levels:** Video podcasts tend to have higher viewer engagement rates, with audiences spending more time on content compared to audio-only formats.
- **Monetization:** Podcasters who incorporate video are more likely to secure sponsorships and ad revenue. A 2024 study by Podnews found that video podcasts earn 25% more on average per sponsorship than audio-only podcasts.

Which Format Should You Choose?

Your choice between video and audio podcasts should be guided by your goals, audience preferences, and resources.

1. **If You're a Beginner:** Start with audio podcasts. They're easier to produce and require minimal equipment. Focus on building

your content and audience before investing in video production.

2. **If Your Audience Prefers Visual Content:** Consider video podcasts if your target demographic is younger or if your content benefits from visual aids.

3. **If Budget Is a Constraint:** Stick to audio if you're working with limited resources. You can always expand to video once you've established your podcast.

4. **If Monetization Is a Priority:** Video podcasts offer more monetization opportunities, but they also require higher upfront investment.

5. **Hybrid Approach:** Some creators successfully combine both formats by producing video content for YouTube and distributing the audio version across traditional podcast platforms. This strategy maximizes reach and accommodates diverse audience preferences.

Final Thoughts

Both video and audio podcasts have their unique advantages and challenges. While audio podcasts offer simplicity and accessibility, video podcasts provide enhanced engagement and monetization opportunities.

The right choice ultimately depends on your goals, audience, and resources. By understanding the pros and cons of each format, you can make an informed decision and create content that resonates with your listeners or viewers.

Whether you choose audio, video, or both, the most important factor is delivering high-quality, consistent content that connects with your audience and keeps them coming back for more.

Chapter 11

How to Start a Podcast Beginner's Guide

Chapter 11 | How To Start a Podcast

Podcasting has exploded in popularity over the last decade, with millions of people tuning in daily to listen to their favorite shows.

Starting a podcast can be an exciting venture, whether you're looking to share your expertise, tell compelling stories, or promote your business.

But for beginners, the process can feel overwhelming.

Fear not—this guide breaks down the steps to help you launch your podcast with confidence and success.

1. Define Your Podcast Concept

The foundation of any successful podcast is a clear and compelling concept. Ask yourself: What's the purpose of your podcast? Who is your target audience? What topics will you cover? Answering these questions will help you carve out a niche and ensure your content resonates with listeners.

Tips:

- Choose a topic you're passionate about or have expertise in.
- Research existing podcasts in your niche to identify gaps or unique angles.
- Write a mission statement to keep your focus clear.

2. Pick a Podcast Format

Podcasts come in various formats, including solo shows, interviews, panel discussions, and narrative storytelling. Decide which format best suits your content and resources.

Popular Formats:

- **Solo**: One host sharing expertise or opinions.

- **Interview**: A host talking to guests, ideal for showcasing diverse perspectives.
- **Co-hosted:** Two or more hosts having discussions, which can add dynamic energy.
- **Storytelling:** Pre-written narratives or investigative series, requiring more planning and production.

3. Plan Your Episodes

Planning your episodes ensures consistency and keeps your content engaging. Create an outline for each episode, including key points, guest questions, and a call-to-action (CTA).

Tips:

- Keep episodes between 20 and 60 minutes, depending on your audience's preferences.
- Plan a launch schedule, such as weekly or biweekly releases.
- Create a backlog of episodes before your launch to avoid gaps in content.

4. Choose Your Podcast Name and Branding

Your podcast's name and branding are critical to attracting listeners. Choose a name that reflects your content and is easy to remember. Design eye-catching cover art that stands out in podcast directories.

Tools:
- Use Canva or Adobe Spark for cover art design.
- Test potential names with friends or colleagues to gauge their appeal.
- Write a short, compelling podcast description that hooks potential listeners.

5. Get the Right Equipment

Investing in good-quality equipment is essential for producing professional-sounding episodes. Thankfully, you don't need a huge budget to get started.

Basic Equipment Checklist:

- **Microphone:** USB microphones like the Blue Yeti or XLR mics like the Audio-Technica ATR2100x are great for beginners.
- **Headphones:** Use closed-back headphones like the Audio-Technica ATH-M20x for clear sound monitoring.
- **Pop Filter:** Reduces harsh popping sounds during recording.
- **Recording Software**: Audacity (free) or paid options like Adobe Audition.

6. Set Up Your Recording Space

A quiet, controlled environment is crucial for high-quality recordings. Find a space with minimal background noise and good acoustics.

Tips for a DIY Studio:

- Use soft furnishings like carpets and curtains to reduce echo.
- Record in a small, enclosed space, such as a closet.

- Use foam panels or blankets to dampen sound.

7. Record and Edit Your Podcast

Once your setup is ready, it's time to record. Practice speaking clearly and naturally, and don't be afraid to do multiple takes.

Recording Tips:
- Warm up your voice before recording.
- Avoid filler words like "uh" and "um."
- Test your audio levels to prevent distortion or low volume.

After recording, use editing software to polish your episodes. Remove long pauses, background noise, and any mistakes. Add intro music and transitions to enhance the listening experience.

8. Host Your Podcast

To distribute your podcast, you'll need a podcast hosting platform. The host stores your episodes and generates an RSS feed, which you'll submit to directories like Spotify and Apple Podcasts.

Popular Hosting Platforms:

- Buzzsprout
- Podbean
- Anchor (free)
- Libsyn

9. Distribute Your Podcast

Submit your podcast to major directories to maximize its reach.

Each platform has its own submission process, but most require your RSS feed, cover art, and podcast description.

Key Directories to Consider:

- Apple Podcasts
- Spotify
- Google Podcasts
- Amazon Music
- Stitcher

10. Promote Your Podcast

Promotion is essential to building an audience. Leverage social media, email marketing, and word of mouth to get your podcast noticed.

Promotion Tips:

1. Share behind-the-scenes content and episode highlights on platforms like Instagram and Twitter.
2. Collaborate with other podcasters to cross-promote episodes.
3. Encourage listeners to leave reviews and ratings to boost visibility.

11. Engage With Your Audience

Building a loyal listener base involves engaging directly with your audience. Respond to comments, ask for feedback, and involve listeners in your content creation.

Ideas for Engagement:

- Create polls or Q&A sessions on social media.
- Read listener comments or questions on your episodes.
- Offer exclusive content or shoutouts for loyal fans.

12. Analyze and Refine Your Podcast

Use analytics tools provided by your hosting platform to track your podcast's performance. Metrics like downloads, listener retention, and geographic data can help you identify what's working and where to improve.

Tips:

- Experiment with different episode formats or topics based on listener preferences.
- Monitor engagement levels to refine your marketing efforts.
- Celebrate milestones, such as hitting 1,000 downloads, to motivate yourself and your audience.

Final Thoughts

Starting a podcast may seem daunting at first, but with proper planning, the right tools, and a clear vision, you can create a show that stands out and builds a loyal following.

Focus on producing high-quality content, engaging with your audience, and continuously refining your craft. The podcasting world is full of opportunities, and now is the perfect time to dive in.

CASE STUDY

Feelin' Hot, Hot, Hot ...

CHAPTER 12

Hot Ones:
Rise of the Viral Podcast

Case study | **Hot Ones**

When *Hot Ones* premiered on March 12, 2015, few could have predicted that a show combining celebrity interviews with escalating spicy chicken wings would capture the world's attention.

Hosted by **Sean Evans**, the show quickly transcended its gimmick to become a cultural staple.

With its ingenious mix of humor, vulnerability, and sheer entertainment, *Hot Ones* carved out a niche in the crowded podcast and web show landscape, amassing millions of devoted fans.

Here, we take a deeper dive into the origins of *Hot Ones*, its most notable episodes, and the metrics behind the podcast's success. We'll also explore why critics, fans, and even its celebrity guests count it as must-see entertainment..

The Origins of *Hot Ones*

Hot Ones began as a quirky idea from **Chris Schonberger**, a producer at Complex Media's food-centric channel, *First We Feast*.

Schonberger, alongside Evans, envisioned a format that would break the mold of traditional celebrity interviews.

Their premise was simple: invite celebrities to eat ten progressively spicier wings while answering questions that range from deeply personal to hilariously absurd.

In an interview with *The Hollywood Reporter*, Schonberger explained, "We wanted to create something that felt different, where the guests could let their guard down.

The spice acts as a truth serum—it's hard to maintain a polished PR persona when your mouth is on fire."

A former journalist, Evans brought his sharp wit and exceptional interviewing skills to the table.

Evans' ability to ask thoughtful questions while maintaining composure (despite the heat from the wings) became one of the show's defining traits.

A Few Episodes That Set the Internet Ablaze

Over the years, *Hot Ones* has hosted a staggering array of celebrities, from A-list actors to viral internet stars. Each episode offers its own unique flavor, but a few stand out in my mind for their cultural impact:

1. Gordon Ramsay (Season 8, Episode 1)

The celebrity chef's legendary episode became an instant classic. Ramsay, known for his fiery temper and culinary expertise, met his match with *Hot Ones'* sauces. His over-the-top reactions, from squirting lime juice into his mouth to applying Pepto-Bismol, have garnered over 121 million views on YouTube as of 2025. This episode solidified the show as a viral juggernaut.

2. Shaquille O'Neal (Season 8, Episode 8)

NBA legend Shaquille O'Neal's mix of bravado and vulnerability became meme-worthy gold. His famous declaration, "I won't make a face," only to immediately succumb to the heat, is a moment that fans continue to share on social media.

3. Paul Rudd (Season 9, Episode 6)

Paul Rudd's charming demeanor and the viral "Look at us" meme from his appearance made this episode one of the most beloved in the series. The wholesome yet hilarious interaction between Rudd and Evans has earned over 65 million views.

4. Billie Eilish (Season 11, Episode 1)

Pop sensation Billie Eilish brought in a younger audience with her candid answers and endearing reactions. Her appearance drove an increase in younger viewers, boosting the show's reach across demographics.

5. President Barack Obama (Special Episode)

In one of the show's most surprising twists, former President Obama appeared on *Hot Ones* to promote his memoir. His thoughtful answers juxtaposed with his calm composure (even with the hottest sauce) demonstrated the show's cultural clout.

The Metrics Behind the Heat

By 2025, *Hot Ones* has grown into a multimedia empire, boasting over 1.5 billion cumulative views on YouTube and millions of podcast downloads. The show's YouTube channel, *First We Feast,* has 13 million subscribers, with *Hot Ones* being its flagship program.

According to data from Tubular Insights, *Hot Ones* averages 3-5 million views per episode within the first week of release. Its most popular episodes exceed 50 million views within a year. Additionally, Spotify and Apple Podcasts rank the *Hot Ones* audio podcast consistently in the top 20 entertainment podcasts globally.

A study by Media Impact Analytics found that *Hot Ones* has an unusually high viewer engagement rate. Over 70% of viewers watch an episode from start to finish, a rarity in the age of short attention spans. The study attributes this to the show's unique format, which combines compelling storytelling with unpredictable moments of hilarity.

Why People Love *Hot Ones*

What makes *Hot Ones* stand out is its ability to humanize celebrities.

As media critic Jason Lynch puts it, "In an industry saturated with polished PR campaigns, *Hot Ones* strips away the veneer. It's not just about the heat; it's about seeing a side of celebrities we rarely get to witness."

Evans himself has commented on this phenomenon. In an interview with *Variety*, he said, "The wings are the equalizer. Whether you're an Oscar-winning actor or a YouTube star, everyone reacts to spice the same way. It levels the playing field and creates a space for genuine interaction."

The format also taps into the internet's love for challenges and extremes. The Scoville Scale, which measures the heat of chili peppers, has become a recurring point of fascination for fans.

The final sauce on the show, "The Last Dab," clocks in at over 2 million Scoville units, creating moments of suspense and drama.

Quotes from Experts and Critics

Hot Ones is a masterclass in blending entertainment with authenticity. Evans has redefined the celebrity interview, turning it into a spectacle without sacrificing substance," says Jessica Carter, a media analyst at New York University.

Schonberger credits the show's success to its relatability: "Everyone knows what it's like to eat something spicy. It's a universal experience, and we've tapped into that in a way that's fun and inclusive."

The Road Ahead

As *Hot Ones* continues to grow, the show is expanding into new territories. A spin-off game show aired on TruTV, and the *Hot Ones* brand now includes a line of hot sauces that have become bestsellers in their category.

The podcast version of the show has also been embraced by fans who want to enjoy the interviews on the go.

Looking ahead, Evans remains focused on innovation. "We're always thinking about what's next," he told *The Verge*. "How can we keep surprising our audience while staying true to what makes *Hot Ones* special?"

Final Thoughts …

Hot Ones is more than just a podcast or web show—it's a cultural phenomenon that has redefined how we consume celebrity interviews.

By blending humor, vulnerability, and a universal love for spice, Sean Evans and his team have created a format that resonates with millions.

Whether it's through viral moments, thoughtful questions, or the sheer spectacle of watching celebrities sweat, *Hot Ones* continues to turn up the heat in the world of entertainment.

With its innovative format and dedicated fan base, *Hot Ones* proves that sometimes, all it takes is a little spice to change the game.

Chapter 13

Monetize Your Podcast:
5 Strategies

Chapter 13 | **Money, Money, Money**

Podcasting has emerged as one of the most dynamic platforms for content creators, offering opportunities to connect with niche audiences in ways traditional media cannot.

Yet, for many podcasters, the transition from passion project to profitable business remains elusive.

Drawing on my 25 years as a public relations professional and media strategist, I'll explore five proven strategies to monetize a podcast, complete with actionable insights and best practices.

1. Leverage Sponsorships and Advertisements

Sponsorships and advertisements are among the most common and lucrative ways to monetize a podcast. By securing partnerships with brands that align with your content and audience, you can generate significant revenue streams.

Why It Works:

Podcast audiences are highly engaged, with a report from Edison Research stating that 54% of podcast listeners say they're more likely to consider purchasing from a brand advertised on their favorite shows. This level of trust translates into tangible results for advertisers.

How to Get Started

Understand Your Audience: Before approaching sponsors, analyze your audience demographics, interests, and behaviors. Tools like Spotify for Podcasters or Apple Podcasts Connect can provide valuable insights.

Create a Media Kit: A professional media kit showcasing your podcast's metrics, audience reach, and engagement levels is essential. Highlight listener demographics, download statistics, and testimonials from past sponsors.

Start Small: If your podcast is new, consider working with smaller local businesses or niche brands within your industry.

Experiment with Ad Formats: Dynamic ad insertion allows you to tailor advertisements to specific audience segments, increasing relevance and revenue potential.

Case Study:

The Smart Passive Income podcast, hosted by Pat Flynn, began monetizing with small sponsorships and gradually scaled to feature larger brands like FreshBooks. By staying true to his audience and only promoting products he genuinely used, Flynn built trust while earning substantial ad revenue.

2. Develop Premium Content and Subscriptions

Premium content models allow loyal listeners to pay for exclusive episodes, ad-free listening, or behind-the-scenes access. Platforms like Patreon, Supercast, and Apple Podcasts Subscriptions make it easy to offer tiered memberships.

Why It Works:
Loyal fans are often willing to pay for extra value, especially if they feel a personal connection with the host. According to Supercast, creators earn an average of $7 per subscriber monthly through premium content.

How to Get Started:

Offer Exclusive Value: Premium content could include extended interviews, Q&A sessions, or access to archives.

Create a Clear Value Proposition: Communicate the benefits of subscribing and ensure the additional content is worth the investment

.

Engage Your Community: Use social media, newsletters, or even your episodes to promote the benefits of subscribing.

Example:

The podcast Chapo Trap House earns over $150,000 monthly on Patreon by offering bonus episodes and direct engagement with their fans. Their success highlights the power of cultivating a loyal and passionate audience.

3. Sell Merchandise

Merchandise is an excellent way to diversify revenue streams while reinforcing your podcast's brand identity. From T-shirts and mugs to stickers and tote bags, branded products can deepen listener loyalty while generating profits.

Why It Works:
Podcast listeners often identify strongly with their favorite shows, making them more likely to purchase branded items. A study by TeePublic found that podcast merchandise campaigns see average profit margins of 30-40%.

How to Get Started:

Design With Your Audience in Mind: Merchandise should resonate with your audience. Incorporate catchphrases, inside jokes, or imagery unique to your show.

Choose a Reliable Partner: Platforms like Printful, Teespring, or Merch by Amazon offer print-on-demand services, reducing upfront costs.

Promote Strategically: Dedicate podcast episodes or social media posts to showcase new merchandise lines.

Example:
The My Favorite Murder podcast turned their quirky humor and loyal fanbase into a thriving merchandise business, selling everything from apparel to enamel pins that reflect their brand's identity.

4. Offer Online Courses, Workshops, or Consulting Services

Many podcasters build authority in their niche, making them ideal candidates for creating educational products or offering consulting services. Whether it's a podcasting workshop, a niche-specific course, or one-on-one coaching, these services can significantly boost your earnings.

Why It Works:

Podcast listeners view hosts as trusted experts, which translates into high demand for educational and consulting services. Research by Podia reveals that educators who incorporate podcasting into their offerings often see a 20-30% increase in course enrollment.

How to Get Started:

Identify Your Expertise: Pinpoint a topic where you can provide actionable value and insights.

Develop a Curriculum: Use tools like Teachable, Kajabi, or Udemy to create and distribute your course.

Promote Through Your Podcast: Dedicate an episode or segment to discussing the value of your educational offerings.

Case Study:

John Lee Dumas of Entrepreneurs on Fire capitalized on his expertise by creating a course on podcasting. His course, *Podcasters' Paradise*, generated over $3 million in revenue by targeting aspiring podcasters eager to learn from a seasoned professional.

5. Affiliate Marketing Partnerships

Affiliate marketing involves promoting a product or service and earning a commission for each sale generated through your referral. It's a low-risk, high-reward strategy for podcasters.

Why It Works:

Affiliate marketing integrates seamlessly into podcast content, allowing you to recommend products naturally while earning income. A study by Statista estimates affiliate marketing spending will surpass $8 billion annually by 2025, highlighting its growth potential.

How to Get Started:

Choose Relevant Products: Promote products or services that align with your podcast's niche and audience.

Use Unique Promo Codes or Links: These tools help track referrals and ensure you're credited for sales.

Be Transparent: Clearly disclose your affiliate relationships to maintain trust with your audience.

Example:

The Tim Ferriss Show generates significant income through affiliate partnerships. Tim promotes products like Audible and Shopify, weaving them into his episodes in a way that feels authentic and engaging.

Final Thoughts:

Building a Sustainable Podcast Business

Monetizing a podcast requires a combination of creativity, persistence, and strategic planning.

While each of the five strategies outlined—**sponsorships, premium content, merchandise, educational offerings**, and **affiliate marketing**—offers unique advantages, the key to success lies in understanding your audience and providing value.

As the podcasting landscape continues to grow, the potential for creators to turn their passion into a profitable venture has never been greater.

By implementing these strategies and staying true to your brand, you can build a sustainable podcast business that not only generates income but also resonates with listeners worldwide.

Chapter 14

Best Practices and Strategies to Gain Visibility for Your Podcast

Chapter 14 | **Get Noticed**

Starting a podcast is an exciting venture, but building an audience and gaining visibility in a crowded marketplace can be challenging.

With over 5 million podcasts available globally, standing out requires more than just great content—it requires a thoughtful and strategic approach to marketing and promotion. Here are the best practices and strategies to help your podcast gain the visibility it deserves.

1. Define Your Target Audience

One of the most critical steps in gaining visibility is understanding who your ideal listeners are. Your podcast content should cater to a specific niche or group of people. Ask yourself:

- Who is your podcast for?
- What problems or interests does it address?
- Where does your audience consume content?

By honing in on a specific audience, you can tailor your marketing efforts to meet their preferences and increase your chances of engagement. For example, a political podcast may focus on young professionals who consume news daily, while a fitness podcast may target busy parents looking for efficient workout tips.

2. Create High-Quality, Shareable Content

Content is king, and the best marketing strategy starts with a podcast that people want to share. Focus on:

- **Strong Hooks:** Open each episode with a compelling story, question, or fact to capture attention.
- **Consistent Quality:** Invest in good recording equipment and editing software to ensure clear audio. Poor sound quality can drive listeners away.
- **Unique Value:** Offer insights, stories, or expertise that your audience can't easily find elsewhere.

- **Engaging Show Notes:** Write detailed episode summaries that include keywords, guest bios, and timestamps. These notes help improve discoverability on search engines.

3. Leverage SEO to Your Advantage

Search engine optimization (SEO) isn't just for blogs—it's essential for podcasts, too. Optimize your podcast for search engines by:

Using Relevant Keywords: Include keywords in your episode titles, descriptions, and show notes. For example, "Top 10 Strategies for Small Business Success" is more searchable than "Episode 3."

Optimizing Your Podcast Name: If your podcast title doesn't clearly describe your niche, add a descriptive tagline. For example, "The Business Builder Podcast: Marketing Tips for Entrepreneurs."

Submitting to Directories: List your podcast on all major directories like Apple Podcasts, Spotify, Google Podcasts, Stitcher, and iHeartRadio.

4. Build a Strong Social Media Presence

Social media is one of the most effective tools to gain podcast visibility. Here's how to maximize your reach:

Create Platform-Specific Content: Use audiograms, quote graphics, and video snippets to promote episodes on Instagram, Twitter (X), TikTok, and Facebook.

Engage with Your Audience: Respond to comments, ask questions, and start discussions about topics covered in your episodes.

Use Hashtags: Research trending and niche hashtags to improve your visibility. For example, #PodcastRecommendations or #TrueCrimePodcast.

Join Communities: Participate in Facebook groups, Reddit forums, or LinkedIn communities relevant to your podcast's niche.

5. Cross-Promote with Other Podcasts

Collaboration is key in the podcasting world. Partnering with other podcasters can help you tap into new audiences. Consider:

Guest Swaps: Invite other podcasters as guests on your show and appear on theirs. This introduces your podcast to their audience.

Ad Swaps: Exchange short ads with podcasts in similar niches to promote each other's shows.

Podcast Networks: Join a podcast network to gain exposure through collective marketing efforts.

6. Encourage Listener Engagement and Sharing

Your existing audience can be your best marketers. Encourage them to help spread the word by:

Asking for Reviews: Politely request that listeners leave ratings and reviews on platforms like Apple Podcasts. These reviews improve your podcast's ranking and credibility.

Creating Shareable Content: Make it easy for listeners to share episodes with friends by providing short, engaging clips or quotes.

Engaging on Episodes: Ask listeners to send in questions or comments to be featured on future episodes. This makes them feel involved and invested.

7. Use Email Marketing to Stay Connected

Email marketing is a powerful way to keep your audience engaged and informed. Build an email list by offering exclusive content, such as bonus episodes, downloadable resources, or early access to interviews.

Weekly Updates: Send newsletters with episode highlights, behind-the-scenes updates, and upcoming topics.

Personal Touch: Use the email to connect directly with your audience, sharing your personal thoughts or asking for feedback.

8. Invest in Paid Advertising

While organic growth is essential, paid advertising can boost your visibility faster. Consider:

Social Media Ads: Platforms like Facebook and Instagram allow you to target specific demographics based on age, interests, and location.

Google Ads: Invest in pay-per-click campaigns to promote your podcast website.

Podcast Apps: Advertise within podcast platforms like Overcast or Spotify to reach people already listening to podcasts.

9. Attend Events and Network

Networking in person or virtually can significantly boost your podcast's visibility:

Attend Conferences: Go to industry events, meet-ups, or podcasting conferences to connect with potential collaborators and listeners.

Host Live Events: Host a live podcast recording or a Q&A session to interact directly with your audience.

Leverage Guest Appearances: Invite notable figures in your niche who have their own audience to amplify your reach.

10. Monitor Your Metrics and Refine Your Strategy

Growth requires constant evaluation. Use analytics to track what's working and what isn't:

Podcast Analytics: Monitor downloads, listener retention, and demographic data on platforms like Spotify for Podcasters or Buzzsprout.

Social Media Metrics: Track engagement, reach, and click-through rates to see which posts resonate most with your audience.

Experiment: Try new formats, topics, or promotional strategies and measure their impact.

Final Thoughts …

Gaining visibility for your podcast takes time, effort, and consistency. By understanding your audience, creating compelling content, leveraging SEO, and strategically promoting your podcast, you'll position yourself for sustained growth.

Remember that every episode is an opportunity to attract new listeners and deepen your connection with existing ones.

CASE STUDY

The Podcast Franchise

Chapter 15

The Joe Rogan Experience

Joe Rogan Experience

In the vast sea of podcasts, one show has managed to not only stay afloat but ride the biggest wave to stardom.

The Joe Rogan Experience (JRE), hosted by comedian, UFC commentator, and self-proclaimed curious mind Joe Rogan, has transcended the podcasting world to become a cultural juggernaut.

What started as a humble experiment in 2009 has turned into a multi-million-dollar enterprise, drawing millions of listeners per episode and sparking conversations worldwide.

The rise of the Joe Rogan podcast is a story of authenticity, eclectic curiosity, and, of course, a few laughs along the way.

Basement Conversations to Global Phenomenon

When Joe Rogan and comedian Brian Redban first launched *The Joe Rogan Experience*, it was more akin to a couple of friends hanging out in a basement with a webcam than a polished production.

Rogan himself has said, "We didn't know what we were doing at all. We were just having fun, and somehow people started listening."

Yet, in that raw and unfiltered format, Rogan stumbled upon something special: authenticity. Listeners were drawn to the unscripted, meandering conversations that felt more like eavesdropping on a fascinating chat than consuming traditional media.

Fast forward to 2020, Spotify signed Rogan to an exclusive licensing deal reportedly worth $100 million.

Reflecting on the deal, Rogan remarked, "It's a strange journey from something that was just me and my buddy talking to something this big."

This watershed moment not only cemented JRE's place in podcasting history but also underscored the medium's growing influence. By this point, Rogan's show was consistently topping charts and amassing billions of downloads, making him a household name and a polarizing figure.

The Secret Sauce: Why JRE Resonates

The success of *The Joe Rogan Experience* can be attributed to a blend of factors that make it unlike any other podcast. First and foremost, Rogan's insatiable curiosity drives the show.

From astrophysicist Neil deGrasse Tyson to comedian Dave Chappelle, and even eccentric entrepreneur Elon Musk, Rogan's guest list reads like a who's who of modern thought leaders and pop culture icons.

"I just love learning," Rogan said in an interview. "I want to talk to people who are smarter than me, funnier than me, or who have lived lives I can't even imagine."

His everyman approach appeals to listeners who appreciate his willingness to dive into complex subjects without pretension.

Fans often cite his marathon-style episodes, which can stretch beyond three hours, as a testament to the depth and nuance he's willing to explore—a stark contrast to the soundbite-driven content dominating traditional media.

"We're not bound by time slots or commercial breaks," Rogan has said. "We can let the conversation go wherever it needs to go."

Humor and Humanity: Rogan's Signature Style

Another key to Rogan's success is his humor and relatability. As a seasoned stand-up comedian, Rogan injects levity into even the densest topics. "The best way to talk about serious stuff is to make people laugh first," he once said. His ability to laugh at himself and his guests fosters a sense of camaraderie.

For instance, in his infamous interview with Elon Musk, when Musk lit up a joint on air, Rogan's bewildered expression—followed by his deadpan, "Is that even legal?"—became an internet meme.

Such moments of unscripted absurdity have endeared him to fans and cemented the podcast's place in pop culture.

Controversy: A Double-Edged Sword

Of course, *The Joe Rogan Experience* hasn't risen to prominence without its fair share of controversy.

Rogan's willingness to host polarizing figures—from conspiracy theorists like Alex Jones to outspoken scientists during the COVID-19 pandemic—has sparked heated debates about platform responsibility and free speech.

Addressing these criticisms, Rogan has said, "I'm not a journalist; I'm just a guy talking to people. My job is to ask questions, not to tell people what to think."

Critics argue that Rogan's massive platform can inadvertently amplify misinformation.

Yet, Rogan remains unapologetic about his approach, emphasizing, "People need to take responsibility for what they consume. I'm not here to spoon-feed anyone."

Metrics of Success

The numbers behind *The Joe Rogan Experience* are staggering.

As of 2023, it is estimated that Rogan averages 11 million listeners per episode.

To put that in perspective, the podcast consistently outperforms prime-time television shows in terms of reach.

Rogan once quipped, "It's crazy to think that more people listen to me talk about hunting than watch cable news."

Beyond sheer numbers, Rogan's influence extends to culture and commerce.

Guests frequently report massive surges in book sales, website traffic, or social media following after appearing on the show—a phenomenon colloquially known as "The Rogan Bump."

For instance, Dr. Rhonda Patrick, a frequent guest and health expert, credited her appearances on JRE with catapulting her research into mainstream awareness.

Why It Resonates with Fans—and the Nation

The rise of *The Joe Rogan Experience* also reflects broader shifts in media consumption. In an era where trust in traditional media is waning, many listeners gravitate toward podcasts as a more authentic and direct form of communication.

"People are tired of being lied to," Rogan has said. "They want real conversations, not soundbites or spin."

Moreover, Rogan's appeal lies in his ability to bridge divides. His guest list—which includes figures across the political, scientific, and cultural spectrum—has made *Rogan* a rare space where diverse viewpoints coexist. For many listeners, it's a refreshing departure from echo chambers and a chance to engage with ideas they might not encounter otherwise.

Lessons from Rogan's Success

The rise of *The Joe Rogan Experience* offers valuable lessons for aspiring podcasters and content creators. Rogan's journey underscores the importance of authenticity, consistency, and adaptability.

By staying true to his interests and creating a space for genuine conversation, he's built a brand that resonates with millions.

As Rogan succinctly put it, "If you're not being authentic, people will smell it from a mile away."

That authenticity, coupled with his curiosity and humor, has made *Rogan* a podcasting phenomenon—and a testament to the power of simply being yourself in a world that often demands conformity.

Final Thoughts

From its humble beginnings as a side project to its current status as a cultural touchstone, *The Joe*

Rogan Experience has redefined what a podcast can achieve.

Love him or hate him, Rogan has undeniably left an indelible mark on the media landscape, proving that curiosity, humor, and a willingness to tackle any topic can resonate far and wide.

For those looking to understand the power of podcasting, there's no better case study than the meteoric rise of Joe Rogan.

Chapter 16

How to Book Celebrities for A Podcast: A Step-by-Step Guide

Chapter 16: **Book Big Names**

Booking celebrities for your podcast can elevate your brand, attract new listeners, and enhance your credibility in your niche.

Whether you're running a political podcast, a show about pop culture, or a niche podcast in business or health, celebrity guests bring star power that can drive engagement and grow your audience.

But how do you convince a celebrity to appear on your show? It may seem intimidating, but with the right strategy and persistence, it's more achievable than you think.

Here's how to book celebrities for your podcast and make their appearances successful.

1. Define the Value You Offer

Before reaching out to any celebrity, identify what value your podcast offers. Celebrities receive countless invitations to podcasts, so you need to stand out. Think about:

Your Audience: Highlight the size and demographics of your audience. For example, if your listeners align with the celebrity's fan base or target audience, mention that.

Your Mission: Share what your podcast stands for. If your mission aligns with the celebrity's values or work, it creates a compelling reason for them to join.

Your Reach: While you don't need millions of listeners, demonstrate that your platform has impact—be it through social media engagement, listener reviews, or loyal followers.

2. Start Small and Build Credibility

If you're new to podcasting, you may not land an A-list guest right away. Start by booking smaller, accessible guests to build your credibility and audience.

Industry Experts: Interview respected figures in your niche who have influence but are more accessible than celebrities.

Rising Stars: Emerging actors, influencers, or authors are often eager to promote themselves and may be more willing to appear on your show.

Past Connections: Reach out to people you already know in your professional or personal network who can provide valuable content.

As you build a portfolio of episodes with interesting guests, you'll have more leverage to attract bigger names.

3. Research the Right Celebrities

Not every celebrity is the right fit for your podcast. Research guests who align with your podcast's theme, audience, and tone.

Relevance: Choose guests whose work or public persona aligns with your podcast's focus. For example, a political commentator may not fit well on a comedy-focused podcast but would be ideal for a news and events show.

Current Projects: Celebrities promoting new books, movies, or initiatives are often looking for publicity opportunities. Timing your request around a launch can increase your chances of success.

Social Alignment: Check their social media activity and public appearances to ensure their values or interests align with your podcast.

4. Craft a Compelling Pitch

Your pitch is critical. It should be short, professional, and tailored to the celebrity or their representative. Here's how to craft an effective pitch:

Start Strong: Lead with your podcast's unique value or a specific reason the celebrity would benefit from appearing. For instance, "I'd love to have you on my podcast to discuss your new book, which aligns perfectly with our audience of [insert demographic]."

Be Personal: Reference their work or recent projects to show you've done your homework.

Highlight Benefits: Explain what's in it for them—whether it's reaching a new audience, promoting a project, or engaging in a meaningful conversation.

Be Clear and Concise: Keep your email or message short and easy to read. Avoid long paragraphs.

5. Reach Out Through the Right Channels

Finding the right point of contact is crucial. Celebrities often have a team that handles their appearances. Consider these options:

Publicists: Many celebrities have public relations teams that manage their media engagements. Search for their publicist's contact information online or on the celebrity's official website.

Agents: Talent agencies often manage celebrity schedules. Contact the agent and explain why their client would benefit from appearing on your podcast.

Managers: Managers handle broader career development and can also connect you with the celebrity.

Social Media: If the celebrity actively manages their social media accounts, you can try sending a direct message. Keep it professional and concise.

6. Be Persistent But Be Respectful

Don't be discouraged if you don't get a response right away. Follow up politely after one or two weeks. Use these follow-up opportunities to:

- Reiterate your value proposition.
- Provide updates on your podcast's growth or recent guest appearances.
- Mention any new projects or milestones relevant to the celebrity.

Persistence shows enthusiasm, but avoid coming across as pushy or desperate.

7. PREPARE (!) for the Interview

Once a celebrity agrees to appear, make the experience as smooth and professional as possible:

Do Your Homework: Research their career, recent projects, and any topics they've spoken about recently. This demonstrates respect and helps you ask meaningful questions.

Communicate Clearly: Confirm the time, format, and duration of the interview well in advance. Provide clear instructions if you're recording remotely.

Send a Prep Sheet: Share a list of topics or potential questions ahead of time so they know what to expect.

8. Promote the Episode Effectively

Celebrity episodes are a major opportunity to grow your audience. Maximize their impact:

Tease the Episode: Share teaser clips, quotes, or behind-the-scenes photos on social media before the episode goes live.

Leverage Their Audience: Ask the celebrity to share the episode with their followers. Provide pre-made graphics or links to make it easy for them.

Highlight Key Moments: After the episode airs, create audiograms or video snippets of the most compelling moments to share online.

9. Build Long-Term Relationships

A celebrity appearance can lead to future collaborations if you foster a good relationship. Send a thank-you note or follow up with updates about how their episode performed. Showing appreciation can open doors for repeat appearances or referrals to other high-profile guests.

Final thoughts …

Booking celebrities for your podcast is a process that requires preparation, persistence, and professionalism.

By offering value, crafting compelling pitches, and maintaining strong relationships, you can secure high-profile guests who elevate your podcast to new heights. Stay patient, stay strategic, and your efforts will pay off.

Chapter 17

A word about affiliate marketing

Chapter 17 | **Marketing Your Podcast**

Podcasting has transformed from a niche medium into a mainstream powerhouse.

With over 464.7 million podcast listeners worldwide as of 2023 and projected growth to 504.9 million by 2024, the opportunities for monetization are vast.

Among the various revenue streams available to podcasters, affiliate marketing stands out as a lucrative and accessible option.

This model enables podcast creators to earn commissions by promoting products or services to their listeners.

 Done right, affiliate marketing can be a win-win for both podcasters and their audience.

Here's a deep dive into how affiliate marketing partnerships can work for podcasts, their benefits, and strategies to maximize earnings.

What Is Affiliate Marketing?

Affiliate marketing is a performance-based marketing model where individuals (affiliates) promote a company's product or service and earn a commission for every sale or action generated through their unique referral link.

Podcasters can integrate affiliate marketing into their episodes by recommending relevant products or services to their listeners.

For example, a tech podcast might promote software tools, while a fitness podcast might partner with health and wellness brands.

Listeners who trust the host's recommendations are more likely to use the referral links or discount codes shared during the episodes.

Why Affiliate Marketing Works for Podcasts

1. Trust and Influence

Podcasts create an intimate connection between hosts and listeners. Unlike other media formats, podcasts often involve deep conversations, personal stories, and a sense of authenticity. This builds trust, making listeners more likely to act on the host's recommendations.

2. Low Barrier to Entry

Affiliate marketing doesn't require an upfront investment from podcasters. Joining affiliate programs is usually free, making it accessible for creators at any stage, whether they're just starting or already have a large audience.

3. Passive Income Potential

Once referral links or discount codes are integrated into podcast episodes, they can continue generating revenue long after the episodes are published. This creates a passive income stream, especially for evergreen content.

4. Scalability

As a podcast grows its audience, the earning potential from affiliate marketing increases. A larger audience means more potential clicks and conversions, leading to higher commissions.

5. Flexibility

Podcasters can choose affiliate programs that align with their niche and audience. Whether it's promoting books, software, fashion, or fitness equipment, there's an affiliate program for almost every industry.

Success Stories: Podcasts Earning Big Through Affiliate Marketing

1. **The Tim Ferriss Show**
   Tim Ferriss, author and podcast host, leverages affiliate marketing by recommending tools and products he personally uses. His detailed reviews and in-depth discussions about these

products make his audience more likely to trust his recommendations, generating significant affiliate revenue.

2. **Smart Passive Income Podcast**

   Host Pat Flynn has built a podcast empire by teaching listeners about online business and passive income strategies. His podcast frequently promotes affiliate products, like website hosting services, which are relevant to his entrepreneurial audience.

3. **My Favorite Murder**

   This true crime podcast integrates affiliate marketing through partnerships with companies like Audible and HelloFresh. By tailoring promotions to their audience's interests, they've achieved high engagement and conversion rates.

Key Strategies to Maximize Affiliate Marketing Revenue

1. Know Your Audience

Understanding your audience's interests, pain points, and purchasing behavior is critical. This ensures the products or services you promote resonate with them and feel natural within the context of your podcast.

2. Promote Relevant Products

Affiliate marketing works best when the promoted products align with the podcast's niche. For instance, a tech podcast might promote gadgets or software, while a parenting podcast could recommend baby products or educational tools.

3. Be Transparent

Listeners value honesty and authenticity. Always disclose affiliate partnerships to maintain trust. Phrases like, "This episode is sponsored by

[Company], and we earn a commission if you use our link," show integrity and build credibility.

4. Provide Value

Don't just mention the product—explain why it's useful. Share personal anecdotes or detailed reviews to show how the product has positively impacted your life. This makes the promotion feel genuine and relatable.

5. Use Unique Links and Discount Codes

Affiliate programs typically provide unique links or discount codes for tracking referrals. Using these makes it easy for listeners to support the podcast while enjoying exclusive deals.

6. Optimize Placement

Strategically place affiliate promotions within your podcast. Mid-roll ads (in the middle of an episode) tend to perform better because they're less likely to be skipped compared to pre-roll or post-roll ads.

7. Cross-Promote on Other Platforms

Extend the reach of your affiliate links by promoting them on your podcast's social media pages, email newsletters, and website. This creates multiple touchpoints for potential conversions.

8. Track Performance

Use analytics tools provided by affiliate programs to monitor clicks, conversions, and revenue. This data helps identify which promotions resonate with your audience and refine your strategy accordingly.

Challenges of Affiliate Marketing for Podcasters

While affiliate marketing offers significant benefits, it's not without challenges:

1. **Dependence on Audience Size**
   The earning potential is closely tied to the podcast's listener base. Smaller audiences may

struggle to generate substantial affiliate revenue initially.

2. **Competition**

   Popular affiliate programs often attract numerous podcasters, making it harder to stand out. Differentiating your promotions through unique messaging is essential.

3. **Slow Results**

   Affiliate marketing is not a get-rich-quick scheme. Building trust and driving conversions take time, especially for newer podcasts.

4. **Program Restrictions**

   Some affiliate programs have specific requirements, such as minimum traffic thresholds or geographic limitations, which may exclude smaller or international podcasts.

Best Affiliate Programs for Podcasters

Here are some reputable affiliate programs that work well for podcasts:

1. **Amazon Associates**
   One of the largest affiliate programs, it allows podcasters to promote millions of products. While commission rates are relatively low, the wide product range makes it versatile.

2. **Audible Affiliate Program**
   Perfect for book-centric or storytelling podcasts, Audible offers commissions for audiobook subscriptions and individual purchases.

3. **Bluehost**
   Popular among tech and business podcasts, Bluehost offers high commissions for website hosting referrals.

4. **Skillshare**

   Educational podcasts can partner with Skillshare to promote online courses, earning commissions for new signups.

5. **HelloFresh**

   Lifestyle and health podcasts often promote HelloFresh, a meal delivery service, offering attractive commissions and exclusive discount codes for listeners.

Final Thoughts

Affiliate marketing offers a lucrative and flexible revenue stream for podcasters. By aligning promotions with their niche, maintaining transparency, and providing value to their audience, podcasters can build trust and drive conversions.

Success in affiliate marketing doesn't happen overnight, but with consistency, creativity, and audience-focused strategies, it can become a significant income source.

Whether you're a seasoned podcaster or just starting, affiliate marketing partnerships can help you monetize your passion while delivering value to your listeners.

With podcasting continuing to grow, now is the perfect time to explore affiliate marketing as a path to success.

Chapter 18

Podcasting Around the World

Chapter 18 | **Podcasting Around the World**

Podcasting has transcended its origins as a niche hobby to become a global phenomenon, connecting audiences and creators across continents.

With millions of podcasts available in multiple languages, the medium has firmly established itself as a cornerstone of modern media. Here, we'll explore podcasting from a global perspective, examining its growth, cultural impact, and the factors driving its popularity worldwide.

A Rapidly Growing Industry

The growth of podcasting on a global scale is nothing short of remarkable. According to a 2023 report by Edison Research, there are over 5 million active podcasts and more than 70 million individual episodes available worldwide.

This expansion reflects increasing interest from both creators and listeners, fueled by advancements in technology and internet access.

The global podcasting market was valued at $14.25 billion in 2022 and is projected to reach $94.88 billion by 2030, according to a report by Grand View Research.

The compound annual growth rate (CAGR) of 27.6% underscores the medium's potential as a lucrative industry.

This growth is evident not only in established markets like the United States but also in emerging markets across Asia, Latin America, and Africa.

Regional Trends in Podcasting

North America

North America remains the largest podcasting market, with the United States leading the charge. Edison

Research's "Infinite Dial" report reveals that 42% of Americans aged 12 and older listened to a podcast in the past month in 2023.

This equates to approximately 140 million monthly listeners.

Canada is also seeing a steady increase in podcast consumption, with 38% of Canadians tuning in monthly, according to The Canadian Podcast Listener report.

Europe

Europe's podcasting market is thriving, driven by countries like Sweden, the United Kingdom, and Germany.

A 2023 study by Statista found that 44% of internet users in Sweden listen to podcasts monthly, one of the highest rates globally.

In the UK, Ofcom reported that podcast listeners grew to 25% of the adult population in 2023, up from 18% in 2020. European podcasts often focus on diverse topics, reflecting the region's rich cultural and linguistic diversity.

Asia-Pacific

Asia-Pacific is one of the fastest-growing podcasting regions, thanks to its large population and increasing internet penetration. China leads the charge, with over 100 million podcast listeners, according to a 2022 report by PwC.

India's podcast market is also expanding rapidly, with KPMG predicting it will reach over 95 million listeners by 2025. Podcasts in the region often blend traditional storytelling with modern formats, catering to diverse linguistic and cultural preferences.

Latin America

Latin America's podcasting scene has exploded in recent years.

A 2023 survey by Voxnest reported that Brazil is the leading market in the region, with 40% of internet users listening to podcasts regularly.

Spanish-language podcasts have also gained popularity, not only within Latin America but also among Spanish-speaking communities worldwide. Platforms like Spotify and iVoox have been instrumental in the region's growth.

Africa

Africa's podcasting industry is still in its infancy but is showing immense potential.

According to the African Podcasters and Voice Artists Association (APVA), podcasting in Africa grew by 58% between 2020 and 2023. South Africa, Nigeria, and Kenya are emerging as key markets.

Podcasts on the continent often address social issues, storytelling, and education, resonating with local audiences.

Factors Driving Global Podcast Growth

Accessibility

The proliferation of smartphones and affordable data plans has made podcasts more accessible than ever. Platforms like Spotify, Apple Podcasts, and Google Podcasts have simplified access, enabling listeners to discover and subscribe to shows with ease.

In regions with limited internet access, creators have adopted innovative solutions, such as sharing episodes via WhatsApp or offline downloads.

Cultural Relevance

One of podcasting's greatest strengths is its ability to cater to niche audiences. Creators around the world are producing content that reflects their unique cultures, languages, and traditions.

For example, in India, regional-language podcasts are gaining traction, while in Africa, podcasts often incorporate local music and storytelling styles.

Monetization Opportunities

The potential for monetization has attracted both independent creators and major media companies to podcasting. Revenue streams such as sponsorships, advertisements, listener subscriptions, and crowdfunding have made podcasting a viable business model.

According to PwC's Global Entertainment and Media Outlook, podcast ad revenue reached $2.4 billion globally in 2022 and is projected to double by 2025.

Corporate and Celebrity Involvement

The involvement of major brands and celebrities has further elevated podcasting's profile. Companies like Spotify, Amazon, and iHeartMedia are investing heavily in exclusive content and high-profile partnerships.

Celebrities like Dax Shepard, Shannon Sharpe, and comedians and *SNL* buddies Dana Carvey and David Spade have also launched successful podcasts, that draw millions of listeners and broaden the medium's appeal.

Challenges and Opportunities

Despite its rapid growth, podcasting faces challenges that vary by region. In some areas, limited internet access and technological barriers hinder adoption.

Additionally, competition among creators is fierce, making it difficult for new podcasts to stand out.

However, these challenges also present opportunities. As podcasting continues to evolve, creators are exploring innovative formats, such as video podcasts and interactive content. Emerging markets offer untapped potential, and advancements in artificial intelligence could revolutionize podcast production and discovery.

The Future of Global Podcasting

The future of podcasting looks bright, with continued growth expected across all regions. As technology advances and more creators enter the field, the medium's reach will only expand. Podcasts have proven their ability to entertain, educate, and inspire, making them a vital part of the global media landscape.

From North America's dominance to the burgeoning scenes in Africa and Asia, podcasting is a truly global phenomenon.

By embracing diversity and innovation, the medium is poised to reach new heights, connecting audiences and creators in ways previously unimaginable.

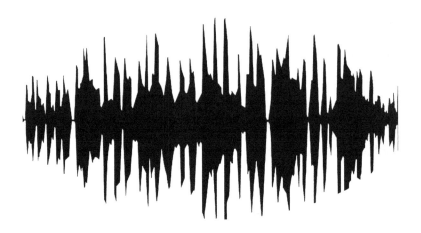

CASE STUDY

Call Her Daddy

Case study | **Call Her Daddy**

In the world of podcasts, few shows have managed to capture the world quite like *Call Her Daddy.*

What began as a cheeky and irreverent take on modern dating has evolved into a cultural juggernaut that redefined how audiences engage with taboo topics.

From its unapologetic humor to its unfiltered exploration of relationships, the show has become a global phenomenon, resonating deeply with fans and stirring conversations nationwide.

But how did *Call Her Daddy* rise from a niche podcast to a multimillion-dollar empire? The answer lies in its unique blend of relatability, audacity, and an uncanny ability to tap into the cultural pulse.

Humble Beginning but Big Aspirations

Call Her Daddy launched in 2018 under Barstool Sports, co-created by Alexandra Cooper and Sofia Franklyn.

The show's premise was simple: two twenty-something women candidly discussing sex, relationships, and their wild experiences in New York City.

Their unabashed honesty and sharp wit immediately struck a chord with millennials and Gen Z audiences who craved real, unfiltered conversations.

In its early days, the podcast was recorded from a makeshift studio and relied heavily on word-of-mouth promotion.

Cooper later joked in an interview, "We didn't even know what SEO was—we just thought if we were loud enough, people would find us!"

And find them, they did.

Within months, the show had climbed the Apple Podcast charts, gaining a fiercely loyal fanbase known as the "Daddy Gang."

Why It Resonates: Humor Meets Relatability

The appeal of *Call Her Daddy* lies in its perfect marriage of humor and relatability.

The hosts' willingness to share their own awkward and outrageous dating stories made listeners feel like they were chatting with their best friends.

From decoding text messages to inventing terms like "gluck gluck 9000" (a cheeky reference to a specific sexual move), the show offered a blend of practical advice and comedic relief that felt fresh and empowering.

In one episode, Cooper described their approach: "We talk about the things you're too embarrassed to bring up at brunch, but everyone's thinking about. That's the magic—it's like ripping the Band-Aid off."

The relatability wasn't limited to dating disasters.

The show also delved into the emotional complexities of relationships, offering listeners a safe space to laugh, learn, and commiserate.

One fan on social media aptly summarized the show's impact: "It's not just about sex—it's about life, empowerment, and learning to own who you are."

The Spotify Deal: A $60 Million Power Move

Call Her Daddy reached a turning point in 2021 when Alexandra Cooper signed an exclusive licensing deal with Spotify for a reported $60 million. This made Cooper one of the highest-paid podcasters in the world, putting her in the same league as the podcast demigod Rogan.

The move underscored not only the show's immense popularity but also its profitability.

Reflecting on the deal, Cooper said, "It's surreal. This show started as two girls sitting in a tiny apartment, and now it's a global platform.

"It's proof that women's voices and stories matter."

The deal wasn't without its drama. Franklyn departed the podcast in 2020 after a highly publicized contract dispute, leaving Cooper as the sole host.

However, the show's momentum continued, with Cooper steering the ship into even greater success.

Under her leadership, *Call Her Daddy* expanded its scope, inviting celebrity guests and tackling broader themes such as mental health, personal growth, and resilience.

The Metrics of Success

The numbers behind *Call Her Daddy* are staggering.

According to Spotify's 2023 metrics, the podcast averages over 3 million downloads per episode, making it one of the platform's most-streamed shows. Its audience skews young, with 75% of listeners aged 18-34 — a demographic highly coveted by advertisers.

The show's success isn't just about downloads; it has also sparked a lucrative merchandise line, including apparel and accessories emblazoned with fan-favorite quotes and inside jokes. In 2022 alone, the *Call Her Daddy* brand reportedly generated over $10 million in merchandise sales.

Moreover, the podcast has wielded significant cultural influence. Terms coined by the show have entered everyday conversations, and its discussions around topics like sexual empowerment and boundary-setting have inspired countless think pieces and debates.

Fan Connection: Building the Daddy Gang

One of the show's standout qualities is its deep connection with fans. Cooper frequently engages with the "Daddy Gang" through social media, Q&A episodes, and live events. This two-way communication fosters a sense of community that traditional media outlets often lack.

Cooper described the relationship in an interview: "I think what makes *Call Her Daddy* special is that it feels like a conversation, not a performance. The fans are part of the journey—they share their stories, and we grow together."

The fanbase's loyalty is evident in their defense of the show during controversies.

When critics accused the podcast of being too risqué or promoting unhealthy relationship dynamics, fans countered that the show's honesty and humor were its greatest strengths.

One listener tweeted, "If you don't get *Call Her Daddy*, you're missing the point. It's about owning your mistakes, laughing at yourself, and refusing to apologize for who you are."

The Show's Impact on Pop Culture

Call Her Daddy has become more than a podcast; it's a cultural touchstone. Its success reflects broader shifts in how young people consume media and engage with taboo subjects.

By normalizing discussions around sex and relationships, the show has helped break down societal stigmas and encourage more open, honest conversations.

As Cooper once said, "If this podcast has taught me anything, it's that vulnerability is powerful. The more we share, the more we realize we're all going through the same crazy stuff."

Lessons from the Rise of Call Her Daddy

The meteoric rise of *Call Her Daddy* offers valuable lessons for aspiring podcasters. Its success underscores the importance of authenticity, relatability, and knowing your audience.

By leaning into what made it unique—raw honesty and humor—it carved out a space in a crowded market and became a voice for an entire generation.

Cooper's advice to creators is simple: "Be yourself. If you try to imitate someone else, you'll lose what makes you special. People connect with realness, not perfection."

Final thoughts …

From its irreverent beginnings to its status as a podcasting powerhouse, *Call Her Daddy* has proven that authenticity and audacity can be a winning combination.

Its impact goes beyond downloads and dollars—it sparked conversations, built communities, and empowered listeners to embrace their messy, beautiful lives.

As Alexandra Cooper continues to steer the ship, one thing is clear: *Call Her Daddy* isn't just a podcast. It's a movement, and it's here to stay.

Chapter 20

Why podcasts fail
10 Common Reasons Podcasts Fail

Chapter 20 : **Why Podcasts Fail**

Podcasting has become an incredibly popular medium for sharing stories, expertise, and entertainment. Yet, for every podcast that breaks into the mainstream, countless others fade into obscurity.

Having worked with many podcasters, I've seen recurring mistakes that lead to podcast failures. Here are the 10 most common reasons podcasts fail and how to avoid them.

1. Lack of a Clear Concept

A podcast without a clear, well-defined concept is doomed to struggle. Listeners need to know what they're getting into when they hit play. If your podcast topic is too broad or unfocused, you risk alienating your target audience. Successful podcasts have a niche and cater to a specific group of listeners.

Solution: Develop a clear mission statement for your podcast. What's your unique angle? Identify your audience and tailor your content to their interests.

2. Inconsistent Publishing Schedule

Listeners crave consistency. Whether it's weekly, bi-weekly, or monthly, sticking to a schedule builds trust and keeps your audience engaged. Many podcasters fail because they release episodes sporadically or burn out after a few weeks.

Solution: Start with a realistic schedule you can sustain. Batch-record episodes in advance to stay ahead.

3. Poor Audio Quality

Listeners will tolerate a lot, but bad audio isn't one of them. Background noise, echo, or low-quality microphones can quickly turn people away.

Solution: Invest in basic podcasting equipment like a quality microphone and use free or affordable editing software. Record in a quiet space to minimize distractions.

4. Lack of Preparation

Some podcasters wing it, thinking they can carry an episode on personality alone. This often leads to rambling, unstructured episodes that lose listeners.

Solution: Outline your episodes before recording. Prepare questions for guests and key points for solo episodes. Having a structure doesn't mean you can't be spontaneous, but it ensures you stay on track.

5. Not Promoting the Podcast

Even the best podcasts need marketing. Many podcasters assume that uploading an episode is enough, but without promotion, it's hard for new listeners to find you.

Solution: Share your podcast on social media, collaborate with other creators, and encourage listeners to leave reviews. Consider joining podcast directories and cross-promoting on platforms like YouTube or blogs.

6. Neglecting Audience Engagement

Podcasts thrive on building communities. If you're not engaging with your listeners, you're missing out on valuable feedback and loyalty.

Solution: Respond to listener comments, emails, or social media messages. Create opportunities for audience interaction, such as Q&A episodes or polls.

7. No Monetization Plan

Many podcasters start with dreams of making money but fail to develop a monetization strategy. Without funding, it can be hard to sustain a podcast over time.

Solution:: Explore options like sponsorships, listener donations, affiliate marketing, or merchandise. Make monetization part of your long-term strategy.

8. Ignoring Analytics

If you're not paying attention to your podcast's performance, you're missing critical insights. Metrics like downloads, listener retention, and demographics can reveal what's working and what isn't.

Solution:: Use podcast hosting platforms that provide analytics. Regularly review the data to refine your content and marketing strategies.

9. Unrealistic Expectations

Building a successful podcast takes time. Many podcasters quit early because they expect instant success and get discouraged when their audience doesn't grow quickly.

Solution: Set realistic goals and celebrate small wins. Focus on creating quality content and building a loyal audience over time.

10. Failing to Evolve

Sticking to the same format and content forever can lead to stagnation. Listeners appreciate growth and innovation.

Solution:: Regularly evaluate your podcast's content and format. Experiment with new ideas, guests, or series to keep things fresh.

Final Thoughts ...

Podcasting is a rewarding but challenging journey. By addressing these common pitfalls, you can increase your chances of building a successful show.

Remember, the key to longevity is a combination of passion, preparation, and perseverance.

If you're serious about podcasting, take the time to develop a strong foundation and learn from the mistakes of others. Your listeners will thank you—and so will your future self.

Chapter 21

Podcast Analytics:
Is Your Podcast Working?
Measuring Success or Failure

Chapter 21 | Analytics

Podcasting has revolutionized the way people consume content, offering an intimate and versatile medium for storytelling, education, and marketing. However, the rapid growth of the podcasting industry has made it more competitive than ever.

While creating engaging content is essential, understanding podcast analytics is the key to measuring its success or identifying areas for improvement. Analytics offer valuable insights into listener behavior, content performance, and audience growth.

Here, we explore the most critical metrics that determine whether a podcast is thriving or failing.

1. Downloads and Streams: The Foundational Metric

Downloads and streams are often the first metrics podcasters consider when evaluating success. A download occurs when a listener saves an episode to their device, while a stream refers to content being played directly from a hosting platform. Together, these numbers indicate the popularity of your podcast and serve as a benchmark for audience reach.

Why It Matters: While downloads and streams are useful indicators of overall performance, they don't tell the full story. A high download count may look impressive, but it doesn't necessarily mean that listeners are engaging with your content.

Industry Standard: According to a 2023 report by Buzzsprout, podcasts that receive over 30 downloads within the first seven days rank in the top 50% of shows. If your episodes consistently surpass this threshold, you're already ahead of the curve.

2. Listener Retention:

The Engagement Metric

Retention metrics measure how much of your episode listeners consume before dropping off. This is a critical indicator of how engaging and relevant your content is.

Why It Matters: Listener retention provides a deeper understanding of your audience's behavior. For instance, if most listeners drop off after the first 10 minutes, it may indicate that your introduction is too long or lacks excitement.

Key Tool: Platforms like Apple Podcasts and Spotify provide detailed retention graphs, allowing you to pinpoint moments where listeners disengage. Use this data to refine your content and maintain audience interest.

3. Audience Demographics: Knowing Your Listeners

Understanding who your listeners are can significantly impact your content strategy. Demographic data includes information like age, gender, location, and device usage.

Why It Matters: Tailoring content to your audience's preferences is vital for growth. For example, if your primary audience is 25-34 years old, you might focus on trending topics or culturally relevant discussions.

Example: According to Edison Research, 56% of podcast listeners in the U.S. are aged 12-34, highlighting the medium's popularity among younger audiences. Knowing this can help you create content that resonates with this demographic.

4. Subscriber Growth: Building Loyalty

Subscribers are listeners who opt to receive new episodes automatically. Tracking subscriber growth over time is an excellent way to measure your podcast's momentum.

Why It Matters: A steady increase in subscribers indicates that your content is resonating and that listeners find it valuable enough to commit.

Pro Tip: Encourage listeners to subscribe at the end of each episode. Consistency in publishing new episodes can also help retain and attract subscribers.

5. Unique Listeners: Expanding Your Reach

Unique listeners refer to the number of distinct individuals who tune in to your podcast over a specific period. Unlike downloads, this metric focuses on the actual number of people engaging with your content.

Why It Matters: Unique listeners provide a clearer picture of your audience size, helping you assess the true reach of your podcast.

Example: If you have 1,000 downloads but only 300 unique listeners, it suggests that your core audience is downloading multiple episodes—a positive sign of loyalty.

6. Episode Completion Rate: Quality Over Quantity

The completion rate measures the percentage of listeners who finish an episode. A high completion rate is a strong indicator of engaging and well-structured content.

Why It Matters: Episodes with high completion rates signal to podcast platforms that your content is valuable, which can improve visibility in search rankings.

Target Benchmark: Aim for a completion rate of 70% or higher. Lower rates may indicate that your episodes are too long or lack a compelling narrative.

7. Listener Acquisition: Growth Trends

Listener acquisition tracks how many new listeners you're gaining over time. This metric helps you evaluate the effectiveness of your promotional efforts.

Why It Matters: A stagnant acquisition rate could indicate that your marketing strategy needs refinement.

Pro Tip: Experiment with cross-promotions, guest appearances on other podcasts, and targeted social media campaigns to attract new listeners.

8. Social Media Engagement:

Extending The Brand

Social media platforms are essential for podcast promotion. Tracking likes, shares, comments, and follower growth can provide insights into how well your podcast resonates outside the audio realm.

Why It Matters: Active engagement on social media helps amplify your podcast's reach and fosters a sense of community among listeners.

Example: Create shareable content like audiograms or behind-the-scenes videos to encourage listeners to promote your podcast organically.

9. Call-to-Action (CTA) Effectiveness

Most podcasts include CTAs, such as asking listeners to leave reviews, visit a website, or support the show on platforms like Patreon. Measuring the response to these CTAs can help gauge audience engagement.

Why It Matters: CTAs provide direct feedback on how invested your audience is. A high response rate indicates strong listener loyalty and interest.

Pro Tip: Keep CTAs simple and actionable. For instance, "If you enjoyed this episode, leave a review on Apple Podcasts" is more effective than listing multiple requests.

10. Revenue Metrics: Monetization Success

If you're monetizing your podcast through sponsorships, ads, or listener donations, revenue metrics are crucial. These include ad impressions, click-through rates, and subscription income.

Why It Matters: Tracking revenue metrics helps you determine whether your podcast is financially sustainable.

Example: A CPM (cost per mille) model, where sponsors pay per 1,000 downloads, is a common monetization strategy. Understanding your average CPM can help you negotiate better deals.

11. Feedback and Reviews: The Voice of the Listener

Listener feedback, whether through reviews, emails, or social media comments, provides qualitative insights into your podcast's impact.

Why It Matters: Positive reviews boost your podcast's credibility and visibility, while constructive criticism helps you improve.

Pro Tip: Encourage listeners to leave honest reviews. Addressing feedback publicly can also strengthen your relationship with your audience.

12. Benchmarking Against Competitors

Comparing your podcast's performance to similar shows in your niche can help you set realistic goals and identify areas for improvement.

Why It Matters: Benchmarking offers context for your metrics, helping you understand what success looks like in your specific genre.

Key Tool: Platforms like Chartable allow you to track rankings and reviews across podcast directories, giving you insights into your competitive position.

Final Thoughts: Analytics Foster Growth

Understanding podcast analytics isn't just about identifying strengths and weaknesses; it's about using data to tell a story.

By interpreting metrics in context and making informed decisions, you can refine your content, attract a larger audience, and achieve long-term success.

As the podcasting landscape continues to evolve, staying attuned to analytics will ensure that your show remains relevant, engaging, and impactful.

Whether you're a beginner or a seasoned podcaster, leveraging these metrics is the key to unlocking your podcast's full potential.

Chapter 22

The Future of Podcasting?

Chapter 22 | **Future or Fad?**

Podcasting has evolved from a niche hobby to a mainstream medium that influences millions of listeners worldwide.

With more than 464.7 million podcast listeners globally as of 2023, the medium continues to grow at a rapid pace, fueled by advancements in technology, shifting consumer habits, and innovative content strategies.

As we look ahead, the future of podcasting appears to be one of expansion, transformation, and opportunity. Here's a deep dive into what the future holds for podcasting, supported by industry insights and data.

1. Continued Growth in Global Listenership

The global podcast audience has seen exponential growth in the last five years, and this trend is expected to continue. Statista projects that by 2028, the number of podcast listeners worldwide will surpass 800 million. This growth is driven by increased smartphone penetration, improved internet access in developing markets, and the rise of audio streaming platforms like Spotify and Apple Podcasts.

In emerging markets, podcasts are becoming a preferred medium for learning and entertainment. Countries like India, Brazil, and Indonesia are experiencing significant increases in podcast adoption as more consumers seek out content in their native languages.

This globalization of podcasting presents immense opportunities for creators to tap into diverse audiences.

2. Diversification of Revenue Streams

The podcast industry's monetization landscape is expanding rapidly. According to PwC, global podcast ad revenues are projected to reach $4 billion by 2024, up from $2 billion in 2022.

While sponsorships and advertising remain the primary revenue sources, podcasters are exploring other avenues, such as subscription models, merchandise sales, and premium content offerings.

Spotify and Apple Podcasts have already introduced subscription options, enabling creators to charge for ad-free episodes, bonus content, and early access.

These models allow podcasters to build sustainable businesses while offering value to loyal listeners. Additionally, innovations in dynamic ad insertion (DAI) technology are enhancing the ability to deliver targeted, localized ads, further boosting revenue potential.

3. Advancements in Podcast Technology

Technology continues to reshape the podcasting landscape. Artificial intelligence (AI) and machine learning are being integrated into podcast production, distribution, and discovery. AI-driven tools like Descript and Adobe Podcast simplify editing by automating tasks such as transcription, noise removal, and even voice synthesis.

Moreover, podcast platforms are investing in personalized recommendation algorithms to help listeners discover new shows. These algorithms analyze user behavior and preferences, creating a more tailored listening experience. For creators, this means increased discoverability and audience growth.

Voice search technology is another game-changer. As smart speakers and voice assistants like Amazon Alexa and Google Assistant become more prevalent, optimizing podcasts for voice search will be crucial. This shift underscores the importance of metadata, keywords, and structured data in podcast descriptions.

4. Rise of Niche and Hyper-Localized Content

While popular shows like "The Joe Rogan Experience" dominate headlines, the future of podcasting lies in niche and hyper-localized content. Listeners are increasingly seeking podcasts that cater to their specific interests, communities, and cultures.

This trend is evident in the growth of podcasts focusing on topics such as true crime, mental health, and regional storytelling.

Brands are also capitalizing on this trend by creating branded podcasts that serve as extensions of their marketing strategies. For instance, Trader Joe's "Inside Trader Joe's" podcast gives customers an inside look at the brand, fostering loyalty and engagement.

5. Interactive and Immersive Podcasting

The integration of interactive and immersive elements is poised to redefine the podcasting experience. Advances in augmented reality (AR) and virtual reality (VR) are paving the way for immersive audio experiences that blur the lines between podcasting and gaming.

Companies like Audible are already experimenting with audio-first storytelling formats that incorporate soundscapes and branching narratives.

Interactive features, such as live Q&A sessions and listener polls, are also becoming more common. Platforms like Spotify have introduced interactive podcast features that allow creators to engage directly with their audiences, fostering deeper connections and loyalty.

6. Corporate and Educational Podcasting

The utility of podcasts extends beyond entertainment. Corporations and educational institutions are increasingly using podcasts as tools for internal communication, training, and learning. Podcasts offer a convenient and engaging way to deliver information, making them ideal for busy professionals and students.

For example, companies are producing internal podcasts to keep employees informed about organizational updates, while universities are using podcasts to supplement course materials. This trend highlights the versatility of podcasting as a medium for knowledge dissemination.

7. Challenges in Content Saturation

As the podcasting space becomes more crowded, standing out will be a significant challenge for creators. With over 5 million podcasts available on various platforms, discoverability is a key concern.

Podcasters will need to invest in marketing, SEO optimization, and cross-promotion to gain visibility.

Additionally, maintaining listener retention will require high-quality, consistent content. The rise of AI-generated content could exacerbate competition, as it lowers barriers to entry but also risks diluting the quality of podcasts.

8. The Role of Podcast Networks

Podcast networks are playing an increasingly prominent role in shaping the industry's future. By pooling resources, networks like Wondery, Earwolf, and Gimlet Media provide creators with access to professional production, marketing, and monetization support.

For listeners, networks offer curated content libraries that make it easier to discover high-quality shows.

9. Podcasts as a Tool for Social Change

Podcasts have proven to be powerful platforms for advocacy and social change. Shows addressing issues such as climate change, racial justice, and mental health are fostering meaningful conversations and inspiring action.

As younger audiences gravitate toward socially conscious content, this trend is expected to grow, positioning podcasts as catalysts for change.

Final Thoughts

The future of podcasting is bright and full of possibilities. With advancements in technology, diversification of revenue streams, and a growing global audience, the medium is set to become an even more integral part of our media ecosystem.

However, creators and brands must adapt to challenges such as content saturation and changing consumer preferences to thrive in this competitive space.

As podcasting evolves, one thing remains clear: its ability to connect, inform, and entertain audiences will continue to make it a powerful tool for communication and storytelling.

CASE STUDY

Community

Chapter 23

Latinx Lens: A Podcast That Speaks to the Heart of the Latino Community

Case study | **Latinx Lens**

In the expanding world of podcasting, certain shows rise to prominence not only because of their content but because of the connection they foster with their audiences.

Latinx Lens, a podcast created by Rosa Parra and Catherine Gonzales, is one such phenomenon.

This podcast has quickly become a touchstone for the Latino community, offering insightful commentary on Latinx representation in film and media while providing a much-needed platform for voices that often go unheard.

Through a mix of humor, passion, and cultural pride, Latinx Lens has carved a unique niche in the podcasting world, resonating deeply with fans across the nation and beyond.

Humble Beginnings

Latinx Lens was born out of a shared passion for film and a desire to highlight the often-overlooked contributions of Latinx creators in Hollywood and beyond.

As Catherine Gonzales once remarked in an interview, "We started this podcast because we wanted to have conversations that we weren't hearing anywhere else. There's so much talent in the Latinx community, and we wanted to shine a light on it."

The podcast's early days were modest, with Rosa and Catherine recording episodes in their homes, armed with little more than a microphone, a laptop, and an unwavering commitment to their mission.

Despite these humble beginnings, their authenticity and passion quickly caught on. Listeners found their discussions both enlightening and entertaining, often punctuated by humorous anecdotes and personal stories that made the hosts relatable.

Why Latinx Lens Has Been Successful

One of the key reasons Latinx Lens has struck a chord with its audience is its unique focus on Latinx representation in media. In an industry where diversity often feels like an afterthought, Rosa and Catherine's in-depth analyses of films, television shows, and the broader cultural landscape offer a refreshing perspective.

Their discussions range from celebrating groundbreaking works like Alfonso Cuarón's *Roma* to critiquing the lack of nuanced Latinx characters in mainstream media.

As Rosa Parra explained, "We're not just talking about films; we're talking about how these films reflect our experiences, our struggles, and our triumphs. That's what makes Latinx Lens more than just a podcast—it's a celebration of our culture and our stories."

It's Funny

While the subject matter is often serious, Latinx Lens never shies away from injecting humor into its episodes. Whether it's sharing behind-the-scenes bloopers or poking fun at Hollywood stereotypes, Rosa and Catherine's banter keeps the tone light and engaging.

This blend of humor and insight has endeared them to listeners, who appreciate the balance between thoughtful critique and genuine fun.

One memorable moment came during their review of a popular blockbuster. Catherine jokingly remarked, "If I had a dollar for every time a Latino character was portrayed as a gardener or a gang member, I could fund my own film studio."

The quip not only drew laughs but also highlighted a pervasive issue in media representation.

Metrics of Success

The success of Latinx Lens can be measured not only in its growing listener base but also in its impact on the conversation around Latinx representation. According to data from Podcast Insights, the show has seen a 150% increase in downloads year over year, with a current average of 50,000 monthly listeners.

Additionally, the podcast boasts a strong social media presence, with over 25,000 followers across platforms like X and Instagram.

Perhaps more telling is the feedback from listeners, many of whom credit the podcast with inspiring them to explore their own cultural heritage. "I never realized how much I craved seeing my culture represented in a positive light until I started listening to Latinx Lens," one fan wrote in a review. "Rosa and Catherine have given me a new appreciation for the power of storytelling."

Quotes from the Rosa and Catherine:

Both Rosa and Catherine have been vocal about the importance of their work and the impact it's had on their lives. In a recent interview, Rosa shared, "We've received messages from people all over the world who tell us that our podcast has made them feel seen and heard. That's the most rewarding part of this journey."

Catherine echoed this sentiment, adding, "When we started Latinx Lens, we had no idea it would resonate on this level. It's a testament to the fact that there's a hunger for stories that reflect the diversity of the human experience."

Expert Opinions

Podcasting experts have taken note of Latinx Lens's success and its potential for continued growth. Jessica Rivera, a media strategist, commented, "Latinx Lens is a prime example of how niche content can find a wide audience when it's authentic and well-executed.

"The podcast's focus on representation fills a significant gap in the market, and I have no doubt it will continue to thrive," she added.

Podcast producer Miguel Torres, said, "What sets Latinx Lens apart is its ability to educate while entertaining. The hosts bring a depth of knowledge and a passion for their subject matter that's truly rare. I wouldn't be surprised to see them branching out into other media formats in the future."

The Road Ahead

As Latinx Lens looks to the future, the hosts remain committed to their mission of celebrating Latinx voices. Plans for live events, merchandise, and even a potential book are all in the works, signaling that this podcast is just getting started.

In the words of Rosa Parra, "We've come a long way, but there's still so much more to do. Our community has endless stories to tell, and we're honored to be a part of that process."

Final Thoughts …

The rise of Latinx Lens is a testament to the power of storytelling and the importance of representation. By shining a spotlight on Latinx creators and their work, Rosa Parra and Catherine Gonzales have created a podcast that not only entertains but also inspires.

Through humor, insight, and a deep love for their culture, they've built a platform that resonates with listeners around the world. As they continue to grow and evolve, Latinx Lens serves as a shining example of what's possible when passion meets purpose.

Chapter 24

Find Your Voice: The Power of Podcasting to Inspire the World

Chapter 24 | Find Your Voice

In a world inundated with fleeting social media posts and endless digital noise, podcasting stands as a beacon of authentic connection and meaningful storytelling.

Whether you're an entrepreneur, a creative thinker, or simply someone with a story to share, podcasting offers a unique platform to amplify your voice, inspire others, and make an impact.

As the legendary broadcaster Edward R. Murrow once said, *"The obscure we see eventually. The completely obvious, it seems, takes longer."* Podcasting, much like Murrow's own storytelling, illuminates those hidden stories that need to be told, connecting humanity in profound and unexpected ways.

If you've ever considered starting a podcast but felt hesitant, this is your sign to begin. Here's why podcasting is one of the most empowering mediums of our time and how you can step into it with purpose and confidence.

Your Voice Matters

Every person has a unique perspective shaped by their experiences, values, and dreams.

Podcasts thrive on diversity of thought and authenticity, making them the perfect medium for anyone willing to speak from the heart.

Author Brené Brown once remarked, *"Vulnerability is the birthplace of innovation, creativity, and change."* Podcasting, at its core, is an act of vulnerability.

Whether you're discussing entrepreneurship, sharing a personal journey, or exploring niche interests, your podcast can serve as a catalyst for change—both for yourself and your listeners.

Remember, you don't need to have all the answers. You simply need to start. Many of the most beloved podcasts began with humble origins: a single microphone, a quiet room, and a passionate storyteller.

The Power of Connection

Podcasting isn't just about speaking—it's about creating a community. When you put your thoughts, ideas, and stories into the world, you invite others to join in the conversation.

Listeners connect with your voice, your message, and your humanity in ways that are deeply personal.

In the words of Maya Angelou, *"People will forget what you said, people will forget what you did, but people will never forget how you made them feel."*

Podcasts have the power to evoke emotion, foster empathy, and inspire action. Whether your goal is to educate, entertain, or empower, your podcast can leave a lasting impression on listeners around the globe.

Overcoming Self-Doubt

One of the biggest barriers to starting a podcast is the nagging question: *"Who am I to do this?"*

The truth is, every successful podcaster has faced this same doubt. But they pushed through, and so can you.

As motivational speaker Les Brown says, *"Shoot for the moon. Even if you miss, you'll land among the stars."*

Podcasting is an opportunity to stretch beyond your comfort zone and discover your potential. It's not about being perfect—it's about being real.

Embrace the imperfections, the awkward pauses, and the learning curve. They're all part of the journey. The key is to start, refine, and grow.

Podcasting as a Platform for Change

Podcasts have become a driving force for social change and cultural conversation. They amplify voices that might otherwise go unheard and create spaces for dialogue around important issues.

Think about some of the most influential podcasts in recent years. Shows like *Serial* brought true crime storytelling to the forefront while sparking discussions about the justice system.

The Happiness Lab with Dr. Laurie Santos transformed scientific research into practical advice for everyday life.

By starting your podcast, you contribute to this powerful tapestry of voices. Your perspective could be the spark that ignites change in someone else's life.

Inspiring Others Through Your Passion

One of the greatest joys of podcasting is sharing what you love with others. Whether your passion lies in technology, cooking, sports, or philosophy, there's an audience out there waiting to hear from you.

As Steve Jobs famously said, *"The only way to do great work is to love what you do."* Your enthusiasm will resonate with listeners and keep them coming back for more. Passion is contagious, and your excitement can inspire others to explore new ideas and possibilities.

Practical Steps to Start Podcasting

Getting started may feel overwhelming, but it doesn't have to be. Here are three simple steps to launch your podcast:

1. **Clarify Your Why**: Determine your purpose for podcasting. Is it to educate, entertain, or share personal experiences? Understanding your

"why" will guide your content and keep you motivated.

2. **Start Small**: Don't worry about having the perfect setup. Many successful podcasters began with basic equipment and upgraded over time. A quality microphone and free editing software like Audacity or GarageBand are enough to get started.

3. **Be Consistent**: Podcasting is a long game. Commit to a regular schedule, whether that's weekly, bi-weekly, or monthly. Consistency builds trust and keeps your audience engaged.

The Time is Now

The podcasting landscape is thriving, with over 5 million podcasts globally and new listeners discovering the medium every day.

It's never been easier—or more exciting—to join this dynamic space.

As the famous proverb goes, *"The best time to plant a tree was 20 years ago. The second-best time is now."*

There's no better time to start your podcast than today.

Inspiration to Keep Going

Podcasting is more than just a medium; it's a movement. It's a way to amplify your voice, connect with others, and leave a legacy.

Each episode you create is a building block in a larger narrative—your narrative.

So, what story will you tell?

As you embark on your podcasting journey, remember the words of Mahatma Gandhi: *"Be the change that you wish to see in the world."*

Your voice matters.

Your story matters.

The world is waiting to hear it.

CASE STUDY

Stand Tall - A Podcast For America

Chapter 25

Interview with Dave Brown:

Behind the Mic of *Stand Tall with Dave Brown*

Case study | Standing Tall in America

Dave Brown is more than just a host—he's a storyteller, advocate, and thought leader with a passion for empowering others.

But most of all, he's a real friend to me.

His show is on Apple Podcasts titled, **Stand Tall with Dave Brown.** *Dave brings years of experience in public speaking, mentorship, and community engagement, and coaching to his show.*

Dave has a wealth of knowledge and a compassionate perspective he brings to every conversation. His ability to tackle tough topics with grace and insight has made Stand Tall with Dave Brown a trusted podcast platform for meaningful dialogue. He's been a trusted podcast partner, a provocative co-host and a loyal friend.

Beyond the podcast, Dave's commitment to making a difference extends to his work in the community, where he continues to inspire others to stand tall in their own lives. His deep faith and unwavering belief in the power of resilience and purpose are the foundation of everything he does.

––––––––––

ROB STAGGENBORG: Dave, thank you so much for joining us today. Your podcast, *Stand Tall with Dave Brown*, has garnered quite a following with its unique blend of political analysis, inspiring stories, sports insights, and reflections on faith and education. To kick things off, can you tell us what inspired you to start the podcast?

DAVE BROWN: Thank you for having me. The inspiration for Stand Tall came from a deep desire to connect with people on multiple levels. I've always been passionate about storytelling and exploring the threads that weave us together as a society. Whether it's politics, sports, or personal perseverance, I wanted a platform where I could not only share my views but also amplify the voices of others who've faced challenges and triumphed. The name Stand Tall reflects resilience, integrity, and the courage to stand firm in our beliefs and values.

RS: Resilience seems to be a recurring theme in your episodes. You often highlight stories of people overcoming adversity. Can you share a particularly memorable story that resonated with you and your audience?

DAVE BROWN: Absolutely. One story that stands out is from an episode featuring a young woman, who overcame incredible odds to pursue her education. She grew up in an underprivileged community where opportunities were scarce, but her determination to succeed was unwavering. Despite financial challenges and personal setbacks, this young lady earned a scholarship to a prestigious university and is now advocating for educational reform in underserved areas. Her story moved me and many listeners because it embodies perseverance and the power of education to transform lives.

RS: Speaking of education, you often reflect on its role in shaping individuals and society. How do you see education intersecting with the other themes in your podcast, like politics and faith?

DAVE BROWN: Education is foundational. It equips people with the tools to engage critically with the world around them, including political and spiritual spheres. On the political front, an informed electorate is crucial for a functioning democracy. Through faith, education fosters a deeper understanding of moral and ethical principles. In one episode, I discussed the intersection of these themes with a pastor who's also a community organizer. We talked about how faith-based initiatives can work alongside educational programs to empower communities. It's all connected—education is the glue that binds these aspects together.

RS: Politics is another core pillar of your podcast. Your analyses are often praised for being balanced and insightful. How do you approach discussing such a polarizing topic?

DAVE BROWN: That's a great question. I approach political analysis with a commitment to fairness and curiosity. I aim to understand perspectives from all sides and create a space for respectful dialogue. In today's climate, it's easy to fall into echo chambers, but I believe in challenging my own views and encouraging listeners to do the same. One strategy I use is bringing on guests with differing opinions. For instance, I had a conservative commentator and a progressive activist on the same episode to discuss healthcare reform. The conversation was spirited but productive, and that's what I strive for.

RS: Your background as a sports coach also shines through in your podcast. How does the world of sports contribute to the themes of perseverance and community that you emphasize?

DAVE BROWN: Sports are a microcosm of life. They teach us about teamwork, discipline, and resilience. Many athletes face tremendous challenges, both on and off the field, and their stories are incredibly inspiring. I've had the privilege of interviewing some remarkable individuals, like a Paralympic athlete who overcame a life-altering accident to become a world champion. Their journeys remind us of the power of grit and determination. Beyond individual stories, sports bring communities together in ways few other things can. Whether it's a local high school game or the Olympics, sports have a unique ability to unite people.

RS: You've mentioned faith as a personal and professional guiding force. How does your own faith influence the content and tone of your podcast?

DAVE BROWN: Faith is the bedrock of who I am, and it naturally influences my perspective. That said, I strive to make the podcast inclusive and welcoming to people of all beliefs. My faith shapes my values, like compassion, integrity, and service, which I hope come through in the stories I choose to share. For example, I recently did an episode on forgiveness, drawing on both personal experiences and broader societal issues. It's amazing how universal some of these principles are, regardless of one's religious or spiritual background.

RS: Your podcast covers such a broad range of topics. How do you decide what to focus on in each episode?

DAVE BROWN: It's a mix of planning and intuition. I keep an eye on current events, but I also listen closely to my audience. Their feedback often inspires new directions. For instance, after an episode on mental health in sports, I received messages from listeners sharing their own struggles. That led to a follow-up series on mental health in various contexts, including education and the workplace. At the end of the day, my goal is to address topics that resonate with people and provide them with value.

RS: What challenges have you faced as a podcaster, and how have you overcome them?

DAVE BROWN: Like any creative endeavor, podcasting comes with its hurdles. Early on, one of the biggest challenges was finding my voice and defining the podcast's identity. There's so much content out there, and it's easy to feel like you have to compete or conform. I learned to stay true to my vision and trust that authenticity would resonate with the right audience. On a technical level, there's always something to learn, whether it's editing audio or navigating distribution platforms. Perseverance has been key, and I've been fortunate to have a supportive team and audience.

RS: What has been the most rewarding aspect of hosting Stand Tall?

DAVE BROWN: Hands down, it's the connections I've made. Hearing from listeners about how an episode impacted them is incredibly fulfilling. For instance, a teacher once told me that she used one of my episodes about perseverance in her classroom to inspire her students. Moments like that remind me why I started this journey. The podcast has also given me the opportunity to meet and learn from extraordinary people, which is a reward in itself.

RS: Looking ahead, what are your hopes and plans for the future of Stand Tall?

DAVE BROWN: I'm excited to continue evolving the podcast. One goal is to expand into live events and community outreach. I want to create opportunities for listeners to engage not just with me but with each other. I'm also exploring collaborations with organizations that align with the podcast's mission, whether it's promoting education, supporting mental health, or celebrating stories of perseverance.

Ultimately, I hope to keep inspiring and empowering people to stand tall in their own lives.

RS: That's a compelling vision, Dave. To wrap up, if you could leave listeners with one message from your podcast, what would it be?

DAVE BROWN: I would say this: No matter what challenges you face, remember that you have the strength to overcome them. Life is full of obstacles, but it's also full of opportunities for growth and connection. Stand tall, stay true to your values, and never underestimate the impact of your story. We all have something to contribute, and together, we can build a better world.

RS: Thank you, Dave, for sharing your journey and insights. *Stand Tall with Dave Brown* is truly an inspiring platform, and we can't wait to see what's next. We want to remind listeners they can like and subscribe to this podcast on Apple Podcasts and Spotify - just search Stand Tall with Dave Brown.

DAVE BROWN: Thank you. It's been a pleasure talking with you. And to everyone listening, thank you for your support. Keep standing tall!

Chapter 26

My Podcasting Gear

Chapter 26 | Rob's World

As a bit of a seasoned media expert, podcast consultant, and content creator with over 25 years of experience, I've cultivated a dynamic approach to podcasting that merges creativity with technical precision.

Podcasting has evolved into a sophisticated medium for storytelling, marketing, and thought leadership, and my personal setup reflects this evolution.

My Go-To Podcasting Gear

At the heart of my podcasting workflow is the **Zoom H2N4** recorder. Compact yet powerful, this device allows me to capture high-quality audio with high quality XLR microphones.

These microphones provide professional-grade sound clarity, ensuring that every voice and sound effect is captured with depth and precision. Whether I'm conducting interviews or recording solo episodes, this setup ensures a seamless recording process.

Once the audio is captured, the next step is editing. For this, I rely on **Final Cut Pro X**. While traditionally known for video editing, Final Cut Pro X has become an indispensable tool in my podcast production.

It enables me to create contemporary, stylized edits with modern, punchy opening music and graphics that engage listeners and viewers from the start.

The flexibility of this software allows me to sequence audio and video files with precision, producing polished episodes that stand out in a crowded market.

When it comes to output, versatility is key. I export my files in various audio and video formats—primarily MP4s and MP3s—to cater to different platforms and audience preferences. From **Spotify** and **Apple Podcasts** to **YouTube, Facebook**, and **X**, each platform has unique requirements, and my approach ensures that my content is optimized for maximum reach and engagement.

Creativity and Innovation in Podcasting

Throughout my 25-year media career, creativity has been my passion. Whether working with clients or organizations, I've consistently brought innovative ideas to the table that drive results.

My approach to podcasting is no exception.

Each project I undertake is tailored to the unique goals and needs of the client. From developing compelling narratives to crafting engaging promotional strategies, I ensure that every aspect of the podcast aligns with the brand's vision and objectives.

For instance, I've helped clients conceptualize podcasts that serve as powerful marketing tools, using storytelling to connect with audiences on an emotional level. By integrating contemporary audio techniques and multimedia elements, I create content that resonates deeply with listeners.

This creative approach not only enhances the quality of the podcasts but also boosts their marketability and potential for monetization.

Helping My Podcast Fam Succeed at Dis

One of the most rewarding aspects of my work is empowering clients to launch and grow their podcasts. By sharing my expertise and proven strategies, I've helped businesses, entrepreneurs, and thought leaders build successful shows that amplify their voices and messages.

Monetization is usually the key goal, and I guide clients through developing sponsorship opportunities, audience engagement tactics, and platform-specific growth strategies.

The result?

Podcasts that not only entertain and inform but also generate revenue and build brand loyalty. **You can totally do this.**

Pushing Boundaries with Creativity

Innovation has always been a driving force in my career. Over the years, I've pushed boundaries and explored new ways to elevate content and engage audiences. Risky at times, but the lessons I've learned. Experience is always valuable.

For example, I've developed unique podcast formats that incorporate live elements, audience interactions, and immersive storytelling techniques.

These creative endeavors not only set my clients apart from competitors but also redefine what's possible in podcasting.

In addition, my background as a radio producer has given me a deep understanding of audio storytelling.

I leverage this experience to create podcasts that are not only technically sound but also rich in narrative and emotional impact.

By combining traditional broadcasting principles with modern digital tools, I offer a hybrid approach that maximizes the potential of each podcast.

Final Thoughts

Podcasting is more than just a medium—it's a powerful tool for connection, creativity, and communication.

My personal podcasting setup, combined with years of experience and a commitment to innovation, allows me to produce content that stands out in today's competitive landscape.

Whether it's through high-quality equipment, cutting-edge editing techniques, or tailored strategies for success, I'm passionate about helping clients realize their podcasting goals.

Together, we can transform ideas into impactful, monetizable podcasts that leave a lasting impression.

Chapter 27

Epic Fails:

Stepping Stones to Success

Chapter 27 | **Epic Fails**

Failure is often seen as the opposite of success, but history shows us that it is more accurately a prerequisite.

On this journey, you will fail. It's part of the process.

From renowned entrepreneurs to groundbreaking scientists, failure has been a critical element in many success stories. With persistence, resilience, and a willingness to learn from setbacks, failures can become powerful stepping stones to greater achievements.

The Role of Failure in Building Success

Failure provides invaluable lessons. When things don't go as planned, the experience often reveals what doesn't work, paving the way for innovation and improvement.

As Thomas Edison famously said during his quest to invent the light bulb: "I have not failed. I've just found

10,000 ways that won't work." His persistence turned countless setbacks into a world-changing innovation.

Psychologists suggest that failure fosters growth by encouraging a mindset that embraces challenges. The concept of a "growth mindset," popularized by Dr. Carol Dweck, emphasizes that viewing failure as an opportunity to learn can lead to long-term success.

When we shift our perspective to see failure as a natural part of the journey, we reduce the fear of taking risks—a crucial ingredient in achieving greatness.

Inspiring Stories of Triumph Through Failure

1. **J.K. Rowling**

   Before becoming one of the most successful authors in history, J.K. Rowling faced a series of crushing setbacks. She was a single mother living on welfare, struggling to make ends meet. When she submitted *Harry Potter and the Philosopher's Stone* to publishers, it was rejected 12 times. Despite these rejections, Rowling persevered, and today, her books have sold over 500 million copies worldwide, making her one of the wealthiest women in the UK.

2. **Oprah Winfrey**

   Oprah's early career was fraught with challenges, including being fired from her first television job because she was deemed "unfit for TV." Instead of giving up, she used this experience as motivation to refine her skills and embrace her authentic self. Today, Oprah is a global icon, known for her media empire and philanthropic efforts, proving that resilience can transform failure into unprecedented success.

3. **Steve Jobs**

   Even Steve Jobs, the co-founder of Apple, faced significant failures. In 1985, he was ousted from the very company he helped create. This public humiliation didn't deter him; instead, it fueled his ambition. Jobs founded NeXT and acquired Pixar, which eventually became a major success. When he returned to

Apple, he revolutionized the company, introducing products like the iPhone and MacBook, which changed the tech industry forever.

Why Persistence Matters

Persistence is the common denominator in stories of success born from failure. It takes grit to continue pushing forward in the face of obstacles and rejection.

A study published in *Psychological Science* found that individuals who perceive failure as an opportunity for growth are more likely to succeed in the long run.

Persistence often leads to breakthroughs when initial efforts fall short. Consider Colonel Harland Sanders, who founded Kentucky Fried Chicken (KFC) at the age of 65.

Col. Sanders was rejected over 1,000 times before his chicken recipe found success, but his unwavering determination eventually built a global fast-food empire.

Strategies for Turning Failure into Success

1. **Learn from Your Mistakes**
   Failure offers a chance to analyze what went wrong. Take time to evaluate the factors that contributed to setbacks and use this knowledge to adjust your approach.

2. **Embrace Resilience**
   Resilience is the ability to bounce back stronger after failure. Developing resilience involves maintaining a positive outlook, focusing on solutions rather than problems, and seeking support from mentors or peers.

3. **Set Realistic Goals**
   Breaking down larger objectives into smaller, achievable goals can make setbacks feel less overwhelming. Celebrate small wins along the way to maintain motivation.

4. **Seek Feedback**
   Constructive criticism can be a goldmine for growth. Don't be afraid to ask for feedback from

trusted sources, whether they're colleagues, friends, or industry experts.

5. **Stay Patient**

    Success rarely happens overnight. Recognize that achieving your goals will likely take time and effort, and stay committed to the journey.

The Broader Impact of Embracing Failure

When society normalizes failure as a part of success, it creates an environment where innovation can thrive.

Organizations like Google encourage employees to take risks and learn from mistakes, fostering a culture of creativity.

Similarly, academic institutions that teach the value of failure help students build the resilience they need to succeed in their careers and personal lives.

Final Thoughts: Success Is Built on the Foundation of Failure

Failure is not the end—it is a beginning. It is a tool that sharpens our skills, a teacher that imparts critical lessons, and a motivator that fuels persistence.

As the saying goes, "The only true failure is giving up."

For those willing to embrace failure with an open mind and a determined spirit, the path to success is not only possible but inevitable.

Whether you're launching a new venture, pursuing a creative passion, or striving for personal growth, remember: failure is not a detour; it's a stepping stone.

————

"I have not failed. I've just found 10,000 ways that won't work."

Thomas Edison

About the Author

My name is Rob Staggenborg, APR, and I am a US-based media strategist, podcast producer, consultant, and content creator whose career spans more than 25 years.

With a multifaceted background in journalism, public relations, academia, and broadcasting, I've built a reputation as a thought leader and innovator in media and communication strategies. I am accredited by the Public Relations Society of America.

My journey through very diverse roles has shaped my unique perspective on storytelling, audience engagement, and branding—skills that have helped individuals, organizations, and brands achieve their communication goals.

A Career Rooted in Journalism

My professional journey began in the newsroom. As a journalist, I honed my ability to craft compelling narratives and uncover stories that resonate with audiences. I tried to bring investigative rigor, keen eye for detail, and dedication to ethical reporting which laid a foundation for my future in media and communication.

My journalism career includes service as a writer and photojournalist for the U.S. Army's *European Stars and Stripes*, where I covered stories that informed and inspired military personnel stationed abroad. My time with *Stars and Stripes* gave me invaluable experience in high-pressure environments and a global perspective on storytelling.

After spending years in journalism, I transitioned into public relations, a field where my storytelling expertise and audience-first approach gave me a distinct edge.

Working as a public relations executive, I managed communication strategies for organizations in higher education, non-profit sectors, and beyond. My ability to develop creative campaigns, manage crises, and connect with audiences on a meaningful level earned respect among my colleagues and clients.

Educator and Mentor

My passion for communication extends to education. As a college professor, I've taught aspiring professionals the nuances of media strategy, public relations, and content creation.

My hands-on approach and real-world insights have made me a strong mentor for students entering the competitive world of media and communications. My impact as an educator goes beyond the classroom—my students often credit me with helping them navigate their careers with confidence and ingenuity..

A Pioneer in Podcasting

My journey into podcasting was a natural evolution of my love for storytelling and communication. Recognizing the medium's potential early on, I became a podcast producer and consultant, helping individuals and organizations launch their own shows.

My expertise in branding, audience engagement, and content strategy has made me an invaluable partner for those who were looking to make their mark in the ever-growing podcasting landscape.

As a podcast producer, I am passionate about content that educates, entertains, and inspires.

My focus on authentic storytelling and strategic content planning has led to successful collaborations with diverse clients, from business leaders and educators to non-profits and creative entrepreneurs.

Creative Leadership in Media

My career has been defined by an ability to adapt to and anticipate changes in the media landscape. From my early days as a radio producer to my work as a columnist and promoter, I have consistently leveraged my skills to stay ahead of trends and create impactful content.

My time as a radio producer gave me an understanding of the power of live, unscripted communication, a skill I carry into my work with podcasts and other digital platforms.

As a columnist and promoter, I have used my platform to amplify important voices and causes, particularly in the non-profit and higher education sectors.

Life in Oregon's Wine Country

I live in Oregon's stunning wine region on the outskirts of the metro Portland region with my wife, Dr. Amanda Staggenborg, and our children. Surrounded by rolling vineyards and picturesque landscapes, I find so much inspiration in the natural beauty of our Pacific Northwest surroundings.

While my professional life keeps me busy, I value my time with family and the sense of community that comes with living in a region known for its charm, creativity and general weirdness.

In addition to practicing public relations, I enjoy exploring Oregon's wine culture, connecting with local artisans, and immersing myself in the region's vibrant storytelling traditions.

This idyllic setting provides a perfect backdrop for my career that has thrived on creativity and innovation.

Recognition and Influence

As an Accredited Public Relations (APR) professional, I have demonstrated my commitment to excellence and ethical standards in the field of public relations. My work has been recognized for its strategic impact and its ability to foster meaningful connections between brands and audiences.

I am not only a strategist but also a thought leader who loves to share insights through articles, podcasts, speaking engagements, and workshops. Hot mic or not, I always tell it like it is. Authenticity is the key here.

My experience and consulting in podcasting, media strategy, and content creation continues to influence professionals across many industries. I seek to inspire others to embrace innovation, to stand tall in times of adversity, and to think outside the box. You do you.

A Legacy of Storytelling and Strategy

My media career is a testament to the power of storytelling and the ability to connect people, inspire action, and drive change. Whether I am helping a non-profit amplify its mission, guiding a client through the podcasting process, or teaching the next generation of media professionals, my work reflects my passion for communication and my belief in its transformative potential.

As media continues to evolve, I remain at the forefront, combining my experience, with my advanced education with a forward-thinking approach.

My legacy as a journalist, public relations executive, educator, and creative strategist ensures that his work will continue to shape the world of media for years to come.

"Literally everybody's got a podcast these days"

"WELCOME TO JESUS JAM, I'M YOUR HOST AND ALSO THE SON OF GOD … TODAY, DELICIOUS RECIPES FOR THOSE DAYS WHEN YOU ONLY HAVE LOAVES AND A FEW FISH, PLUS LAZARUS ON RISING FROM THE DEAD …"

Chat GPT image